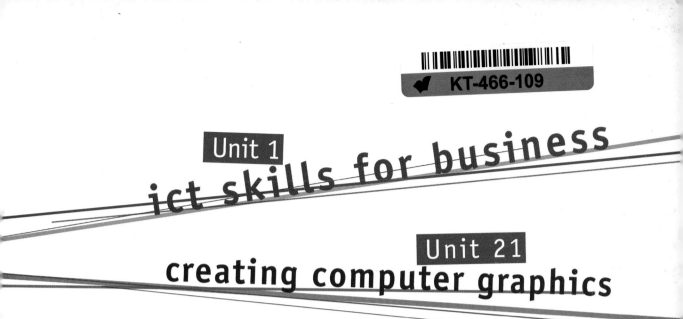

Unit 1
ict skills for business

Unit 21
creating computer graphics

Steve Cushing

Graham Manson

Anne Kelsall

Ruksana Patel

Consultant: Keith Parry

OCR level **2**
Nationals
ict

www.harcourt.co.uk

✓ Free online support
✓ Useful weblinks
✓ 24 hour online ordering

01865 888070

PAYNE-GALLWAY
From Harcourt

Payne-Gallway is an imprint of Harcourt Education Limited, a company incorporated in England and Wales, having its registered office: Halley Court, Jordan Hill, Oxford OX2 8EJ. Registered company number: 3099304

www.harcourt.co.uk

Text © Graham Manson & Steve Cushing 2007

First published 2007

12 11 10 09 08 07
10 9 8 7 6 5 4 3 2

British Library Cataloguing in Publication Data is available from the British Library on request.

ISBN 978 1 905292 11 0

Edited by Liz Cartmell
Designed by Kamae Design
Produced and typeset by Sparks, Oxford – www.sparks.co.uk
Cover photo/illustration © Steve Shott
Printed and bound in China through Phoenix Offset

Acknowledgements
Microsoft product screenshots reprinted with permission from Microsoft Corporation.

Adobe product screenshots reprinted with permission from Adobe Systems Incorporated.

Screenshots of the Google home page and search results page which appear on pages 31 and 32 are copyright Google Inc. and contain Google Brand Features that are trademarks of Google Inc.

Screenshots of the BSD Rescue website on pages 33 and 34 are reprinted courtesy of Cody Harris, Webmaster, Belgian SheepDog Rescue.

Every effort has been made to contact copyright holders of material reproduced in this book. Any omissions will be rectified in subsequent printings if notice is given to the publishers.

Websites
The websites used in this book were correct and up-to-date at the time of publication. It is essential for tutors to preview each website before using it in class so as to ensure that the URL is still accurate, relevant and appropriate. We suggest that tutors bookmark useful websites and consider enabling students to access them through the school/college intranet.

Ordering Information
Payne-Gallway, FREEPOST (OF1771),
PO Box 381, Oxford OX2 8BR
Tel: 01865 888070
Fax: 01865 314029
Email: orders@payne-gallway.co.uk

Contents

Series Introduction

Introduction

This book is one of a series of books that has been designed to guide you in your work for the OCR Level 2 Nationals in ICT. Each book covers two units and explains the skills and concepts that are needed for each. It also sets out in detail how to create a portfolio to achieve a **Pass**, **Merit** or **Distinction** for each assessment objective.

ICT skills for business and *Creating computer graphics* cover the assessment objectives as set out in Units 1 and 21 of the specification.

How to use this book

The book is divided into two sections which guide you through each assessment objective as set out by OCR for Units 1 and 21. Every chapter helps you to understand how you would build evidence for your portfolio through clearly identified scenarios, helpful tips and structured activities using step-by-step instructions. At every stage clear guidance is given as to the level of evidence required for a **Pass**, **Merit** or **Distinction** so that you are able to plan your own progress effectively.

Each student book in the series is further supported by data files for use with some of the activities. These are available for download at the Payne-Gallway website www.payne-gallway.co.uk.

UNIT ①

ICT Skills for Business

In this unit you will cover the following...

➔ **AO1** Demonstrate good working practices with files, directories, folders and sub-folders

➔ **AO2** Download information from the Web and send and receive email messages

➔ **AO3** Create a business presentation using presentation software

➔ **AO4** Create a variety of business documents using word processing or DTP software tools and facilities

➔ **AO5** Create and use a simple business spreadsheet

➔ **AO6** Manipulate a business database using enter, sort and search

Introduction to Unit 1

Unit 1 is the only compulsory unit that you must undertake when working towards your OCR Level 2 National qualification(s) in ICT. It forms the foundation for all other units in the qualifications suite as it looks at the skills and capabilities expected in an office environment.

You will be expected to use a range of standard software applications, including word processing, spreadsheets, database and presentation software. You will have used many of these packages as part of your work at Key Stage 3 but you will now be developing these skills in such a way that you could use them in a business environment

There are six assessment objectives (AOs) in this unit. Although they will all be assessed separately, it is possible that evidence of the work you do for them, especially AO1 and AO2, may be assessed through later AOs as well. Your completed tasks for each AO will form evidence for your portfolio which will be assessed by the exam board. It may include paper copies of your work and/or electronic copies on a floppy disk, memory stick or CD-ROM. You should keep your portfolio organised from the beginning, choosing a suitable folder structure.

Unit 1 is written for Microsoft 2003 applications. It can be used with other versions of these applications although some screenshots and methods may not exactly match these versions.

The activities provided in each of the AOs are examples of how you might approach tasks through the software applications. However, for your portfolio, you will need to create evidence based on scenarios that you or your teacher or tutor have decided upon. The portfolio builder at the end of each AO aims to show you how you may use your learning from each AO in your own project.

CHAPTER ①

➔ *Assessment Objective 1*

Demonstrating Good Working Practices with Files and Directories

Overview:

In this chapter, you will learn how to save and organise your files as well as how to copy, delete and move files and how to create shortcuts to enable you to be more efficient. All of these skills are vital in a working environment.

Assessment Objective 1 is all about developing good working practices when working with computers and evidence of what you learn in this assessment objective should be seen throughout your work in the rest of Unit 1. Good working practice includes, for example, building suitable directory structures, using appropriate filenames, editing files and backing up work. Making sure you know how to do these things well will make you much more efficient when using computers. This assessment objective, therefore, provides a useful guide that you could refer back to when setting up your own directory structures for the work in your portfolio.

In order to complete the activities in this chapter you will need access to a number of additional files. These files are contained in the Chapter 1 Resources zip file which can be downloaded from the OCR Nationals in ICT (Units 1 and 21) Student Resources page on the Payne-Gallway website: www.payne-gallway.co.uk.

- **My Files (folder)**
- **Invoices (folder)**

How this assessment objective will be assessed...

- You will need to produce screenshots for each task you undertake. Where you have changed a filename or folder, you will need to show a screenshot both before and after you make the change.
- For a **Pass,** you will need to provide evidence of the use of appropriate filenames and folder structures. You will also need to provide evidence of your ability to password protect files. You will create, and provide evidence of your ability to create, shortcuts. You will need to provide evidence of backing up files to a removable medium. Alongside the requirements listed for **Pass** level, for a **Merit** you will provide evidence of deleting, copying and moving files. You will also need to produce evidence of your ability to locate and open files from a range of sources, to backup and restore files from a removable medium and to create a shortcut to a program. Alongside the requirements listed for **Pass** level, for a **Distinction** you will need to demonstrate that you use appropriate filenames. You will also need to provide evidence of your ability to rename and password protect files, use search facilities and create, edit and delete shortcuts.

Skills to use...

You will need to:

- save files and rename files and folders
- organise your files and folders
- create new folders and sub-folders
- create and delete shortcuts
- move and copy files and folders
- delete files and folders
- password protect your files
- search for files
- back up your files.

How to achieve...

Pass requirements

P1 You should set up at least two directories.

P2 You should save some files in appropriate locations using appropriate filenames.

P3 You should be able to password protect files.

P4 You should locate and open existing files that you have saved in their directories.

P5 You should backup files onto a removable medium.

P6 You should create shortcuts to at least one directory and one file.

Merit requirements

M1 You should create an appropriate directory structure with at least two main directories, each containing at least two subdirectories using appropriate names.

M2 You should save most files in appropriate locations using appropriate filenames.

M3 You should demonstrate the ability to password protect files.

M4 You should locate and open existing files from a range of sources.

M5 You should provide evidence of at least one instance of deleting, copying and moving files and directories.

M6 You should backup and restore files from a removable medium.

M7 You should create shortcuts to at least one program, directory and file.

Distinction requirements

D1 You should create an appropriate directory structure with at least two main directories, each containing at least two subdirectories using appropriate names.

D2 You should save all files in appropriate locations using appropriate filenames and provide evidence of at least one instance of deleting, copying, moving and renaming files and directories.

D3 You should demonstrate the ability to password protect files.

D4 You should locate and open existing files, using search facilities of operating systems software where necessary.

D5 You should backup and restore files from a removable medium.

D6 You should create, edit and delete shortcuts to at least one program, directory and file.

Choosing appropriate names for your files and folders

Most people don't think very carefully about what to call their files when they save them, but filenames are important. Imagine how difficult it would be to find a file again if you saved lots of files with the same name!

Figure 1.1: *Filenames are important!*

The method you use to name your files is a personal choice – there is no right or wrong way – but it is worth remembering that you may need to find the file again at a later date. Once you have developed your own naming system, it is important to use it consistently.

> **⓵TIP**
>
> Only use a full stop between the name and extension. Avoid using
> ? ‹ › \ : * | ' ^

Your filenames should tell the user about the contents of the file so that you don't waste time opening lots of different files to find the one you want.

Give files precise, specific names and include a **version number** or date if necessary. You could include the date the document was produced in your filename; you can then search for all documents produced in a specific time period.

Key terms

> **Version number**
>
> A version number gives a unique reference number to each copy of your files.

Letter to Fred v2
My CV draft
My CV final version
Notes from meeting 02-06
business presentation
My accounts 2006

Figure 1.2: *Good examples of filenames.*

File extensions

Your computer will automatically add an extension to the filename, but it may not always be displayed. The file extension defines the particular type of file it is: for example, a word processing file created in Microsoft Word has the extension .doc, and a spreadsheet created in Excel has the extension .xls. File extensions tell your computer what type of file it is. This helps the computer to open the correct application when you click on the file.

Other common file extensions are shown below:

Extension	Name	Content
.pdf	Document Format	Documents – text and graphics
.rtf	Rich Text Format file	Text
.txt, .text	Text file	ASCII text
.bmp	Windows Bitmap Graphics	Graphics
.gif	Graphic Interchange Format	Graphics
.jpg, .jpeg	Joint Photographic Experts Group	Graphics – bitmap image format
.mpg, .mpeg	MPEG	Audio and Video
.tif, .tiff	Tagged Image Format File	Graphics (inc. scans and faxes)
.wav, .wave	Waveform Audio	Audio
.ppt	PowerPoint Presentation	Text and graphics

Extension	Name	Content
.exe	**Executable file**	**Programs**
.js	**JavaScript source code**	**Code**
.zip	**Compressed Archive File**	**Multiple file formats**
.gz, .gzip	**Compressed Archive File**	**Multiple file formats**
.htm, .html	**HyperText Markup Language**	**Websites (text, graphics, audio, video, code)**

Renaming folders and files

Activity 1: Renaming a folder...

In this activity you will:

● rename a folder using a right click.

If you have not already done so, download the student resources for this chapter from the Units 1 and 21 student resources page on the Payne-Gallway website: www.payne-gallway.co.uk.

▶ Find the folder called My Files.

▶ Double click to open this folder.

▶ Find a sub-folder called **New Folder**.

▶ **Right-click** on the folder called **New Folder**.

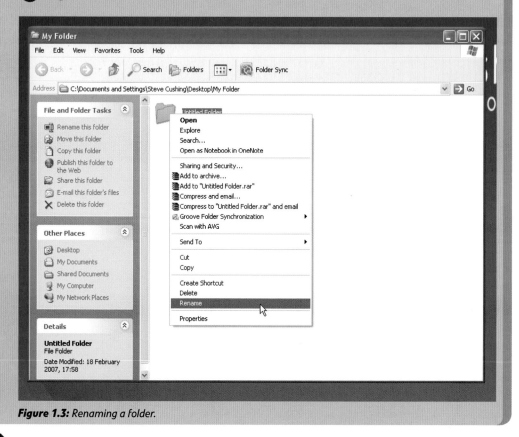

Figure 1.3: *Renaming a folder.*

(▶) Choose **Rename** from the context menu.

(▶) Rename your folder by typing the name **Lesson 1 work** in the name box.

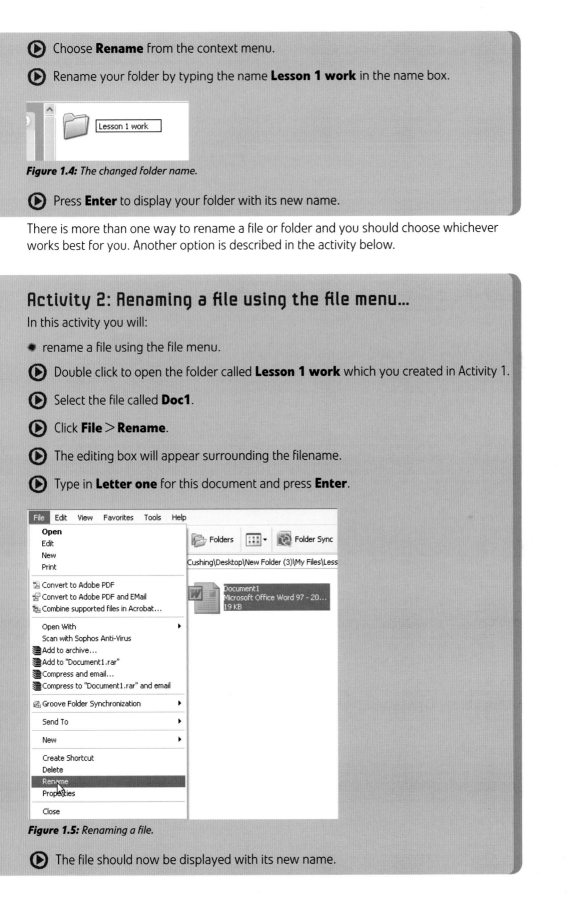

Figure 1.4: *The changed folder name.*

(▶) Press **Enter** to display your folder with its new name.

There is more than one way to rename a file or folder and you should choose whichever works best for you. Another option is described in the activity below.

Activity 2: Renaming a file using the file menu...

In this activity you will:

● rename a file using the file menu.

(▶) Double click to open the folder called **Lesson 1 work** which you created in Activity 1.

(▶) Select the file called **Doc1**.

(▶) Click **File** > **Rename**.

(▶) The editing box will appear surrounding the filename.

(▶) Type in **Letter one** for this document and press **Enter**.

Figure 1.5: *Renaming a file.*

(▶) The file should now be displayed with its new name.

A file that is open in a software application can be saved under a different name by choosing **Save As** from the **File** menu. If you want to save an update to a document and overwrite the original you use **Save**. If you want to save a copy of the original you use **Save As**.

Activity 3: Saving a file using SaveAs...

In this activity you will:

● save a file using the **SaveAs** function.

▶ Go to the **Lesson 1 work** folder and find the file called **Doc2**.

▶ Double click on the document to open it in a word processing program.

▶ Click **File** then **Save As**.

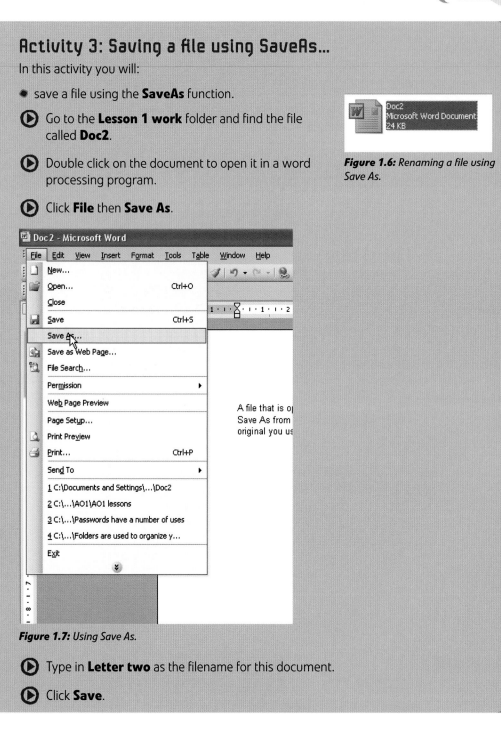

Figure 1.6: Renaming a file using Save As.

Figure 1.7: Using Save As.

▶ Type in **Letter two** as the filename for this document.

▶ Click **Save**.

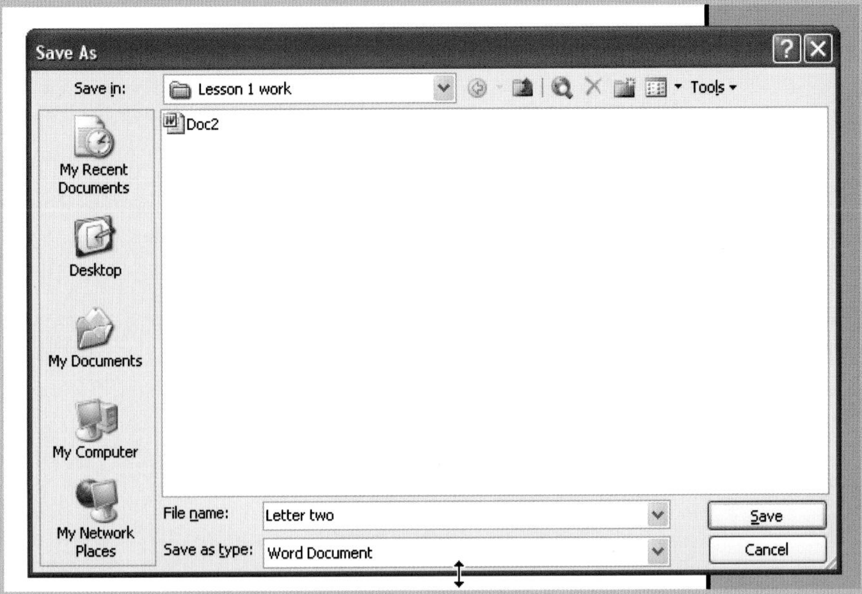

Figure 1.8: *Renaming a file.*

Version control

Sometimes you need to have more than one version of a document because you need to keep a record of the changes made to it. When you have lots of documents it is very easy to select the wrong one. It is important that you know which is the most up-to-date version.

The way you achieve this is to have something called version control; this is where you give a new number to each version of the document each time you save it. This can be done manually or you can set your computer to do this automatically.

For example a first draft of a letter could be called Letter one, the second draft could be called Letter two, etc. After you have saved several versions of your work, you can go back and review and delete the earlier versions.

Figure 1.9: *Saving versions of files.*

File management

Understanding the need for an organised folder structure

Are you a tidy person or do you leave things scattered everywhere?

Being organised at school, college or work makes it easier to work efficiently. Computers cannot change you into a tidy person but they can help you to organise your work.

Good file management means that you can easily find what you're looking for, even if you're looking for it years later.

Sometimes the computer will automatically store files in certain folders in order to keep itself organised. However, when you create new files, you must decide which folders to put them in to keep them organised.

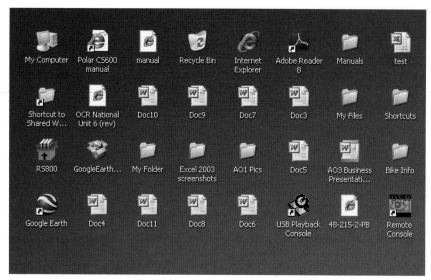

Figure 1.10: *Organising files.*

The folder pictured above (shown viewed by icon and name) is disorganised; it is very difficult to sort through its items. When you organise your files, you can use any system you like, but remember that the goal of organising your files into folders is so that you can find the work as quickly and easily as possible.

To make it easier for you to find files, hard disks are organised into **directories**. Another name for a directory is a folder. Without folders it would be virtually impossible to keep track of all the files that are found on even the smallest system. Just imagine how confusing it would be if you saved your English homework in your mathematics folder by mistake. So for businesses, which can create large numbers of files, it is essential that people create folder structures with recognisable and sensible names so that documents can be retrieved easily and quickly.

Key terms

Directory (or folder)

A group of files, sometimes referred to as a folder, usually represented in a tree structure.

Figure 1.11: *A directory tree.*

As your number of files increases, you will need to create specific folders for your different projects and store the related files in the appropriate folders. For example, you might want one folder for work-related documents, like your portfolio, another for music files and another for your photos.

Creating a folder

Creating a folder is a fairly simple process, as shown in the activity below.

Activity 4: Creating a folder...

In this activity you will:

● create a new folder.

▶ Right click anywhere on an empty part of your desktop.

▶ Select **New** and then click **Folder**.

▶ A new folder with the default name New Folder will be created on the **Desktop**.

▶ Type a new name for the folder and then press **Enter** on the keyboard.

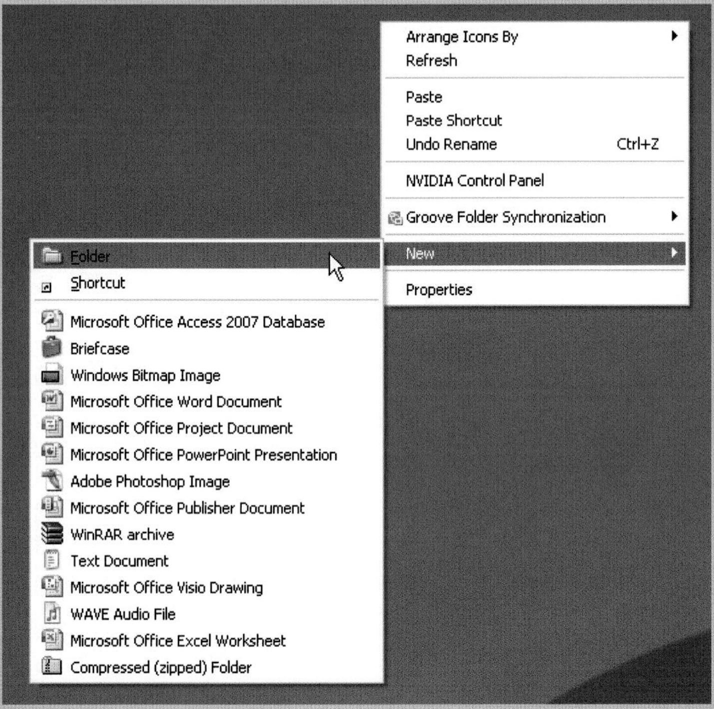

Arrange Icons By	▶
Refresh	
Paste	
Paste Shortcut	
Undo Rename	Ctrl+Z
NVIDIA Control Panel	
🗐 Groove Folder Synchronization	▶
New	▶
Properties	

📁 Folder
🔲 Shortcut
Microsoft Office Access 2007 Database
Briefcase
Windows Bitmap Image
Microsoft Office Word Document
Microsoft Office Project Document
Microsoft Office PowerPoint Presentation
Adobe Photoshop Image
Microsoft Office Publisher Document
WinRAR archive
Text Document
Microsoft Office Visio Drawing
WAVE Audio File
Microsoft Office Excel Worksheet
Compressed (zipped) Folder

New Folder

Figure 1.12: Adding a new folder.    *A New Folder icon.*

Creating a sub-folder

The procedure for creating folders and sub-folders is exactly the same. The only difference is that sub-folders are created within folders that already exist.

Activity 5: Creating a sub-folder...

In this activity you will:

● create a new sub-folder.

▶ Double click the folder you have just created in Activity 4.

▶ Right click in any blank area of the folder window.

▶ Select **New** and then click **Folder**.

▶ A new sub-folder with the default name **New Folder** will be created inside your folder.

▶ Type a new name for the folder and then press **Enter** on the keyboard.

As well as creating a new folder structure, you may find that you need to reorganise an existing one. You can move a file or folder to a different place on your computer by selecting it and dragging it to its new location. If the two locations are on the same drive, the file or folder will be moved. If the two locations are on different drives, the file will be copied.

Organising files into folders

Each folder can hold a different collection of documents which can be both files and folders. You can also separate your folders into groups – these are called sub-folders (folders within folders).

For example, a folder called 'Invoices' might contain further folders called '2004'and '2005', which each contain a variety of related files. Separating your folders like this means that your folder structure can be displayed in such a way that you can easily see the main sections of it. We call this a hierarchical system or tree structure.

Figure 1.13: *Creating sub-folders.*

Most computer file configurations use a tree structure. The tree has one trunk (on stand-alone computers, it is usually labelled C :).

Hard Disk Drives

Local Disk (C:)

Figure 1.14: *A trunk.*

Activity 6: Organising files into folders...

In this activity you will:

● organise related files into folders.

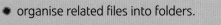 Double click the folder called **Invoices**. The folder contains a range of invoice files. (You should have downloaded this folder at the start of this chapter.)

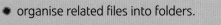 Using the skills you have learnt in Activities 4 and 5, group the files into appropriate folders and sub-folders.

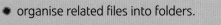 Take a screen print of your new folder structure.

Viewing files

It is often useful to change the way that you view items inside your folders according to the information that you want to know about each file at a glance. For example, the **Thumbnails view** is useful if you are searching through images, or the **Details view** is useful if you want to look at the date you last modified a file. This can be helpful if you have forgotten the name of the file but have an idea about the time you would have last viewed it. The **Tiles view** shows the size of the file as well as the software version and the **Icons** and **List views** are different ways to display the title and software application information.

To look for yourself, go to the **View** menu and choose from the list of options.

Figure 1.15: Choosing viewing options.

Figure 1.16: View by tiles.

Figure 1.17: View by list.

> **① TIP**
> It is important to save your work at regular intervals to avoid losing data if the computer crashes or loses power.

Shortcuts – creating, editing and deleting them

One very useful function that your computer has is the ability to provide shortcuts to files, folders or programs that you use all the time.

Shortcuts are are small files containing a link to the location of another folder or file on your computer. A shortcut can be placed anywhere on your system, the best place is on your **Desktop** or somewhere else that is easily accessible.

Key terms

Desktop

The screen or background appearance of a computer.

Shortcuts are identical in appearance to the icons they represent, except that they have a little arrow in the lower left-hand corner.

Using shortcuts to files and folders saves time and helps you to work more efficiently. In addition, shortcuts take up very little memory space.

A shortcut icon.

Creating shortcuts

Activity 7: Creating a shortcut...

In this activity you will:

● create a shortcut to a file, folder or program.

Method 1

To create a shortcut on the **Desktop** to a file, folder or program:

▶ Right click an open area on the **Desktop**, point to **New**, and then click **Shortcut**.

▶ Click **Browse**.

▶ Locate the program, file or folder to which you want to create a shortcut, click the program, file or folder, click **Open**, and then click **Next**.

▶ Type a name for the shortcut. When the **Finish** button appears at the bottom of the dialog box, click it.

Method 2

To create a shortcut to a program:

▶ Click **Start**, point to **Programs**, and then right click the program you want to create the shortcut to.

▶ Click **Create Shortcut**.

▶ The shortcut is now at the end of the **Programs** list. For example, if you created a shortcut to Microsoft Excel, to find that program, click **Start**, and then point to **Programs**. You will find the shortcut, named '**Microsoft Word** (2)' (without the quotation marks), at the bottom of the Program list.

▶ Drag the shortcut to the **Desktop**.

Activity 8: Creating a shortcut to other objects and editing a shortcut...

In this activity you will:

- create a folder shortcut on the **Desktop**
- change the appearance of a shortcut.

▶ Use **My Computer** or **Windows Explorer** to locate the object to which you want to create a shortcut.

▶ **Right-click** the object and then click **Create Shortcut**.

▶ Drag the new shortcut to the **Desktop**.

To change the appearance of a shortcut:

▶ Right-click the folder shortcut.

▶ Select **Properties** from the properties box.

▶ Select the Shortcut tab.

▶ Click **Change Icon**.

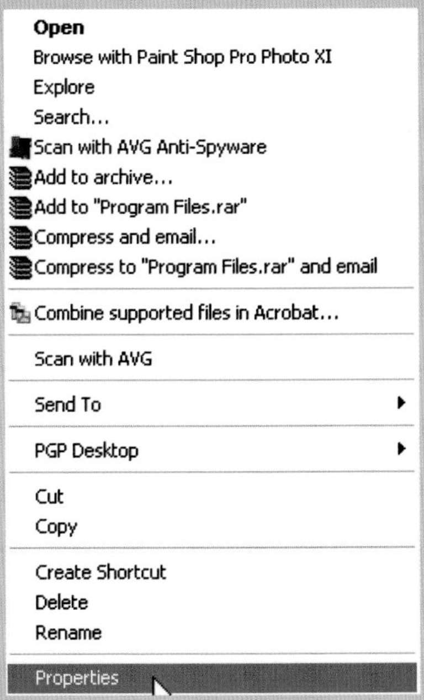

Figure 1.18: *Shortcut properties.*

Figure 1.19: *Change icon.*

▶ Choose an icon from the window.

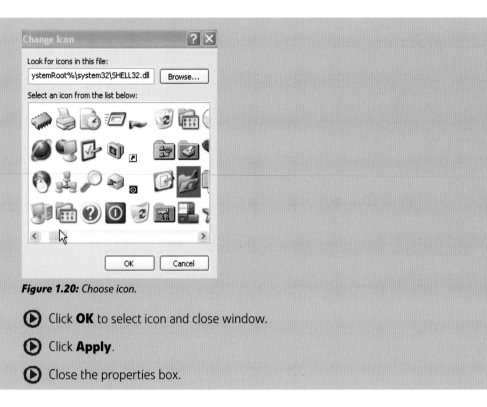

Figure 1.20: *Choose icon.*

▶ Click **OK** to select icon and close window.

▶ Click **Apply**.

▶ Close the properties box.

Deleting shortcuts

Some shortcuts are automatically created when you install programs. You may decide that these are unnecessary.

Activity 9: Deleting a shortcut...

In this activity you will:

● delete a shortcut

▶ Right click the shortcut that you have just created and then...

▶ Click **Delete**.

▶ Alternatively, you can drag the shortcut to the **Recycle Bin**.

> ⊘ **TIP**
> Deleting shortcuts does not remove the original file or program.

Moving and copying files and folders

You can move a file to a different place on your computer by clicking on the file and dragging it to its new location. If the two locations are on the same drive, the file will be moved. If the two locations are on different drives, the file will be copied.

Copying a file creates an identical version of the same file.

Activity 10: Copying files and folders...

In this activity you will:

● copy a file or folder.

▶ Click the file or folder you want to copy.

▶ On the **Edit** menu, click **Copy to Folder**.

▶ Locate the folder into which you want to copy the item.

▶ Click **Copy**.

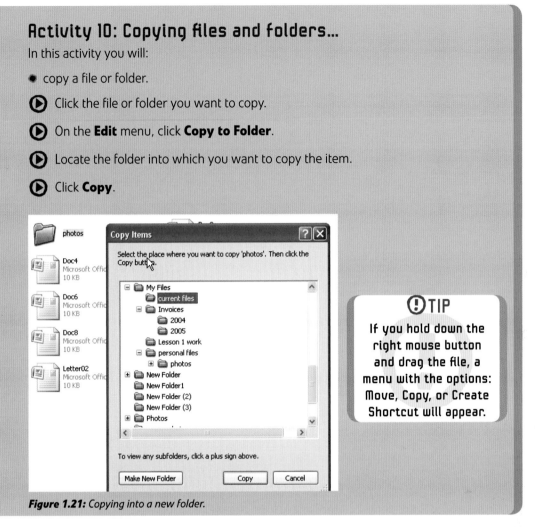

> **①TIP**
> If you hold down the right mouse button and drag the file, a menu with the options: Move, Copy, or Create Shortcut will appear.

Figure 1.21: *Copying into a new folder.*

Activity 11: Moving files and folders...

In this activity you will:

● move a file or folder.

▶ Click the file or folder you want to move.

▶ On the **Edit** menu, click **Move to Folder**.

▶ Locate the folder where you want to move the item.

▶ Click **Move**.

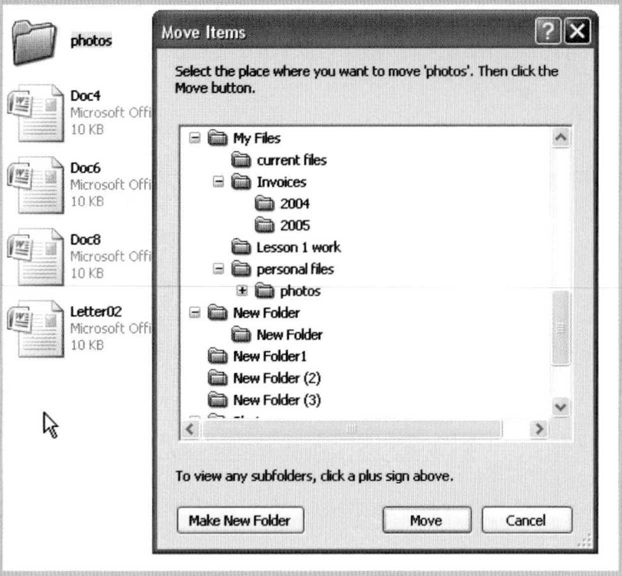

Figure 1.22: *Moving a file or folder.*

TIP

You may also move files by selecting them and dragging them to another folder or sub-folder.

Deleting files and folders

It's a good idea to look through your files and folders regularly and check if there are any that you no longer need. If you are absolutely sure that you don't need a file or folder, you can delete it. This keeps your desktop 'tidy' and stops it becoming cluttered with files and folders that you don't use anymore.

Activity 12: Deleting files or folders...

In this activity you will:

- delete a file or folder.

1. Right click the file or folder to be deleted.
2. Click **Delete**.
3. Click **Yes in the Confirm File Delete** or **Confirm Folder Delete** window.

Alternatively, you can drag the file or folder to the **Recycle Bin**.

Keeping work safe

One of the most common problems faced by students is losing their work. Keeping your work safe is crucial. Most people have experienced the frustration of losing important work on their computer but imagine losing a piece of work that was part of your portfolio. It is your responsibility to ensure that you take all necessary steps to protect your files from loss. Teachers and tutors will not accept this as an excuse for not completing your portfolio!

Businesses are especially careful about making sure that files are not lost because this can affect their performance. They often have employees who are responsible for ensuring that all systems are adequately safeguarded.

Files can be lost for a number of reasons:

- There could be a hardware fault, such as a failure of the computer's hard drive.
- **External storage media** can get lost or damaged.
- Files may accidentally or deliberately be deleted or overwritten.
- **Viruses** can infect computers and destroy all the files.
- Other disasters such as fires, earthquakes and flooding may destroy the computer and all of its files.

Fortunately there are lots of ways you can protect your files.

Key terms

External storage media

A drive that is connected to the computer and can be easily unplugged.

Viruses

A computer virus is a computer program that can copy itself and infect a computer without permission or knowledge of the user.

> ⊘TIP
>
> Try to make a password more secure by combining two or more words together. Remember to change your password regularly.

Password protecting files

If you share a computer or system with someone else you might want to limit access to certain files. You can password protect your files so that they cannot be altered, deleted or completely overwritten. Businesses use this facility when they want to allow employees access to information in files but not the ability to change it. Often this is so that any changes can be channelled through one person who can then keep an overall view of the information in the file.

When you select a password:

- choose one that is at least five characters long
- use letters and numbers
- choose one that you can remember.

Never:

- write down a password where others can find it
- use your name, nickname, date of birth or the name of a close relative or pet.

Activity 13: Password protecting a file...

In this activity you will:

- create a password to protect a file
- create a password to modify a file
- remove a password.

To create a password to protect a file:

▶ Open the file.

▶ On the **Tools** menu, click **Options** and then click **Security**.

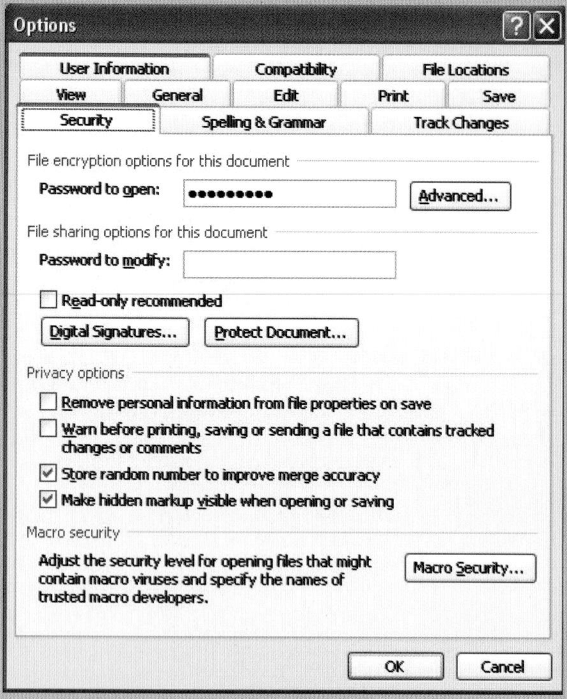

Figure 1.23: *Password protecting a file.*

▶ In the **Password to open** box, type a password, and then click **OK**.

▶ In the **Re-enter password to open** box, type the password again and then click **OK**.

To create a password to modify your file:

▶ In the **Password to modify** box, type a password and then click **OK**.

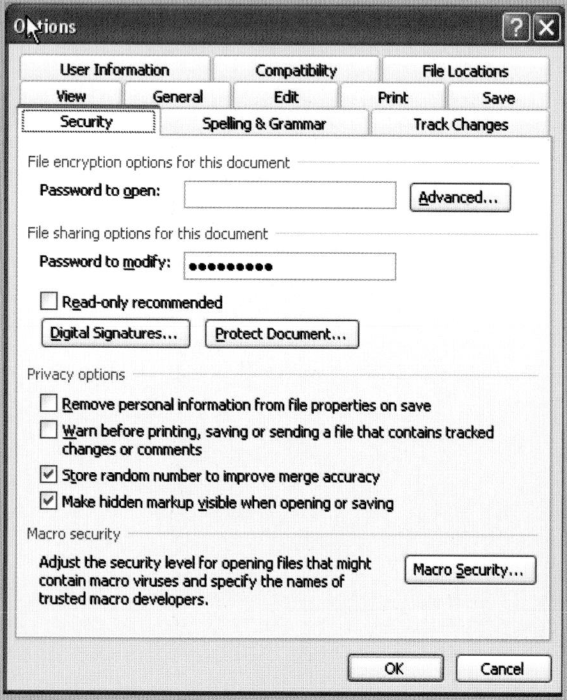

Figure 1.24: *Using a password to modify a file.*

▶ In the **Re-enter password to modify** box, type the password again and then click **OK**.

Confirm Password ☒

Reenter password to open:

●●●●●●●●●

Caution: If you lose or forget the password, it cannot be recovered. (Remember that passwords are case sensitive.)

[OK] [Cancel]

Figure 1.25: *Confirming a password.*

To remove a password:

▶ Open the document.

▶ Enter the password.

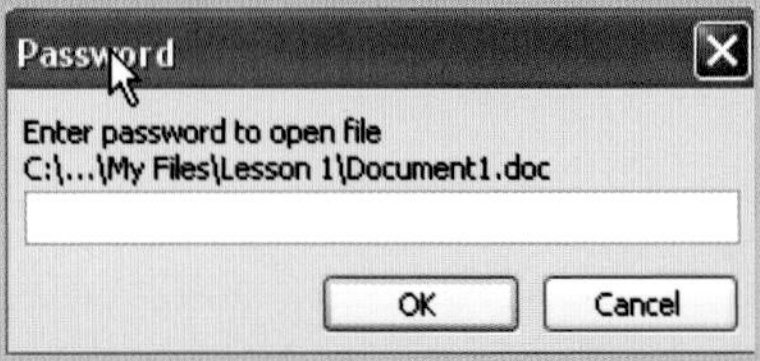

Password 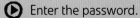 ☒

Enter password to open file
C:\...\My Files\Lesson 1\Document1.doc

[   ]

[OK] [Cancel]

Figure 1.26: *Entering a password.*

▶ On the **Tools** menu, click **Options** and click the **Security tab**.

▶ In the **Password to open** box or the **Password to modify** box highlight the asterisks that represent the existing password.

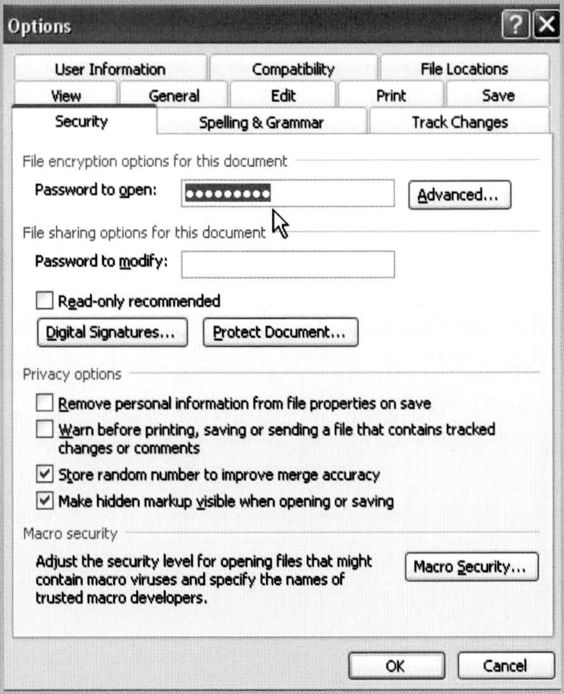

Options [?][X]

User Information	Compatibility	File Locations
View	General	Edit	Print	Save
Security	Spelling & Grammar	Track Changes

File encryption options for this document

Password to open: [●●●●●●●●] [Advanced...]

File sharing options for this document

Password to modify: [   ]

☐ Read-only recommended

[Digital Signatures...] [Protect Document...]

Privacy options

☐ Remove personal information from file properties on save

☐ Warn before printing, saving or sending a file that contains tracked changes or comments

☑ Store random number to improve merge accuracy

☑ Make hidden markup visible when opening or saving

Macro security

Adjust the security level for opening files that might contain macro viruses and specify the names of trusted macro developers. [Macro Security...]

[OK] [Cancel]

Figure 1.27: *Removing a password.*

Then do one of the following:

▶ To remove the password, press **delete** and then click **OK**.

▶ To change the password, type the new password and then click **OK**.

If you changed the password, re-enter the new password and then click **OK**.

Searching for files

You can easily search for files stored on your computer.

Activity 14: Finding a file...

In this activity you will:

● use **File Search** to find a file containing specific text
● use **File Search** to find a file based on one or more properties.

To find a file from within a Microsoft program:

▶ On the standard toolbar select the **File** drop-down menu.

▶ On the **File** menu, click **File Search**.

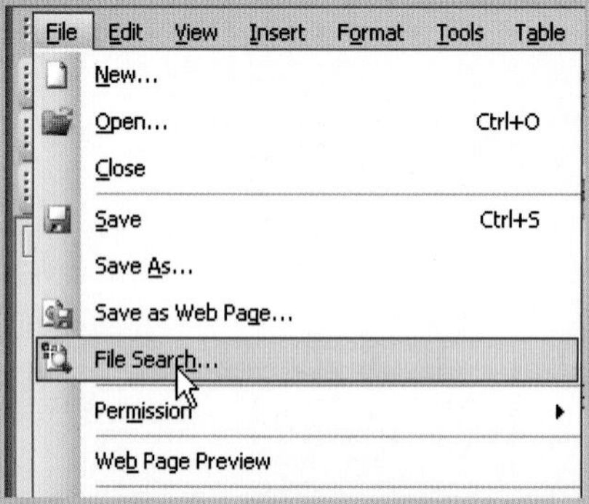

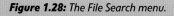

Figure 1.28: The File Search menu.

▶ In the **Search Text** box, type the text you want to search for.

▶ Select one or more drives, folders or mailboxes.

▶ To search everywhere select **Everywhere**.

▶ To find all types of files select **Anything**.

▶ Click **Go**.

Figure 1.29: Basic File Search.

Figure 1.30: Advanced File Search.

To find a file based on one or more properties:

▶ Click on the **Advanced File Search**.

▶ Enter one or more criteria.

▶ To search everywhere select **Everywhere**.

▶ To find all types of files select **Anything**.

▶ Click **Go**.

> **!TIP**
>
> Type a question mark (?) to match any single character in your search text, or type an asterisk (*) to match any number of characters.

You can also search for files using the Microsoft Windows operating system.

▶ Click on the main **Start** menu.

▶ Select **Search**, and then **For Files or Folders...**

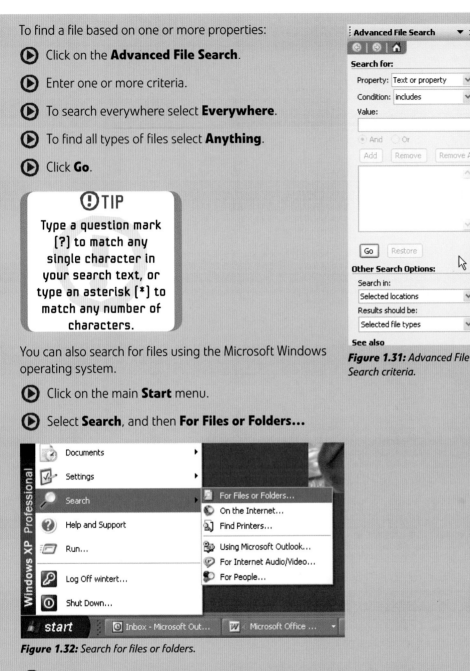

Figure 1.31: *Advanced File Search criteria.*

Figure 1.32: *Search for files or folders.*

▶ By selecting All Files and Folders from the Search Results window you can then search for files by **All or part of the file name** or **A word or phrase in the file**. You can also choose where on your computer you want the search to take place by selecting a location from the drop down list under **Look in:**

▶ Click **Search**.

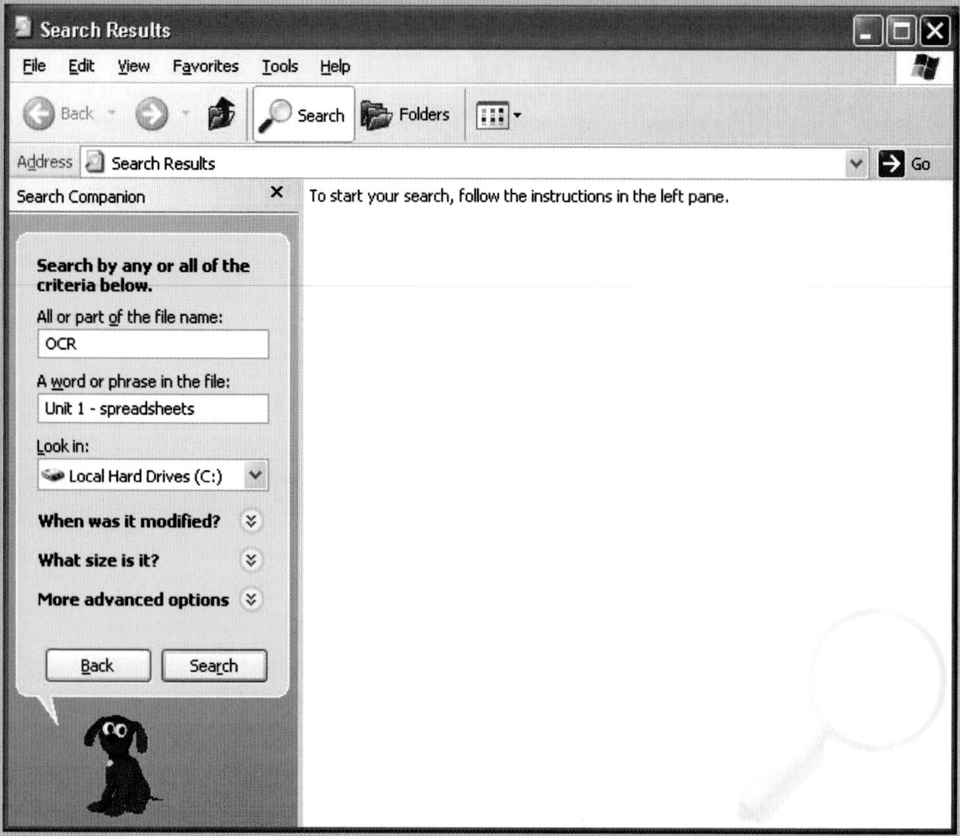

Figure 1.33: *Entering search criteria in the Search Results window.*

Backing up files

If your computer was destroyed, what information would you need to recover? Make a list of all the important files on your computer, for example, your important documents, emails, music files, digital photos, etc.

A backup file is a copy of a data file that is held externally to your computer. For example, you might hold the backup files on a CD-ROM or on a different server. In businesses, the backup files are also held in a different building to the original data file in case of fire or theft. The backup file is restored if the original data file becomes unusable due to file corruption or a system failure such as a hard drive crash.

Backing up your files is the best all round security for your **data**. Backups can protect your data from hardware problems, hackers, user error and natural disasters such as power cuts and lightning strikes.

Key terms

Data

Raw data are numbers, characters and images to be converted into a form usable by a computer.

Backing up data on a regular basis is vital so that files are not lost. While all computer experts recommend that you make regular backups, there is less advice about how you should do it. To keep data safe you should have a backup plan to meet your particular needs.

The answers to these questions will help you to create a suitable plan:

- How often should you back up your files?
- How many files should you back up?
- What media should you back them up on?
- What you should do with the backup files?

When devising a plan you should consider the value of the data, the amount of data, how often you are likely to change the data and what equipment you have to back up the data.

Choose the most suitable backup media for your needs. You can back up your data to a floppy disk, CD or DVD, USB drive, zip drive, external hard drive or to a remote backup site over the Internet.

When you back up data, it will be backed up as it exists on the computer. It is important to check the files first to make sure they are virus free (otherwise your backup will also be infected).

Test your backup by making sure you can restore your files from your backup copy. This will ensure that you have backed up all your work correctly. There is nothing more frustrating than discovering that your backup files are blank because you did not correctly carry out the backup procedure.

Activity 15: Backing-up files to a removable storage medium...

In this activity you will:

- Use the **Back-up** wizard to back-up your work to a removable storage medium

▶ In the Start menu choose **All Programs**, then click **Accessories** then click **System Tools**, then click **Backup**.

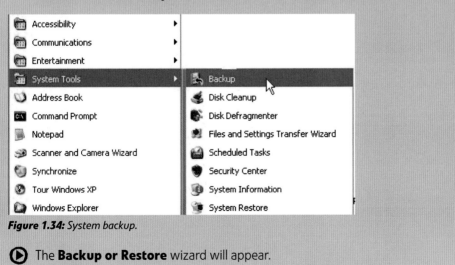

Figure 1.34: *System backup.*

▶ The **Backup or Restore** wizard will appear.

▶ Click **Next**.

▶ Select the radio button next **to Back up files and settings**.

▶ Click **Next**.

▶ Click the radio button next to Let me choose what to back up.

Backup or Restore Wizard ☒

What to Back Up
You can specify the items you want to back up.

What do you want to back up?

○ My documents and settings

   Includes the My Documents folder, plus your Favorites, desktop, and cookies.

○ Everyone's documents and settings

   Includes every user's My Documents folder, plus their Favorites, desktop, and
   cookies.

○ All information on this computer

   Includes all data on this computer, and creates a system recovery disk that
   can be used to restore Windows in the case of a major failure.

◉ Let me choose what to back up

[< Back] [Next >] [Cancel]

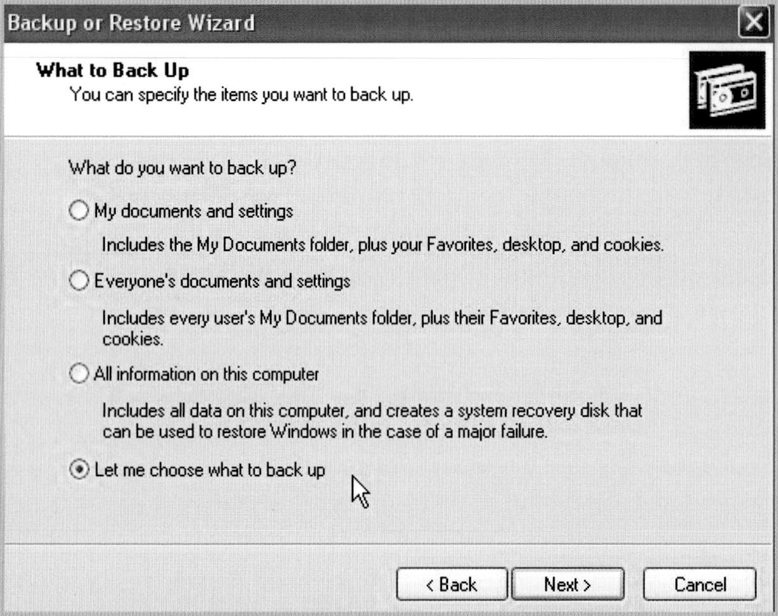

Figure 1.35: What to backup.

▶ Click **Next**.

▶ Tick a file or folder from the list.

▶ Click **Next**.

▶ Choose a destination from the list available or click **Browse** to navigate to a removable disk or external hard drive.

▶ Type a name for your backup.

▶ Click **Next** to see a summary of your backup details.

Figure 1.36: Backup summary.

▶ Click **Finish** to start your backup.

▶ A **Backup Progress** information box will appear.

Figure 1.37: Backup Progress.

▶ Close the box when the backup is complete.

Retrieve files from a backup

All backups should be clearly labelled to ensure that you can retrieve the data at a later date. Make sure you label your backup files with enough detail to indicate the content of each file (see the file naming section on pages 5–9 for more information).

Keep multiple (**incremental**) backups of your most important files from different time intervals – this is sometimes referred to as 'generational' backup so if you keep three generations of backup files this would be grandfather/father/son.

Store your backups safely. It is best to keep a backup copy of files in a secure location, for example, in a locked drawer or a fireproof safe. Ideally, backups should be stored away from the computer, in case of a fire, theft or flood. Backing up online also stores your data offsite in a secure manner.

Activity 16: Restoring files

In this activity you will:

- Use the **Restore Files** wizard to back-up your work to a removable storage medium.

▶ In the Start menu choose **All Programs**, then click **Accessories** then click **System Tools**, then click **Backup**.

▶ The Backup or Restore wizard will appear.

▶ Click **Next**.

▶ Select the radio button next to **Restore files and settings**.

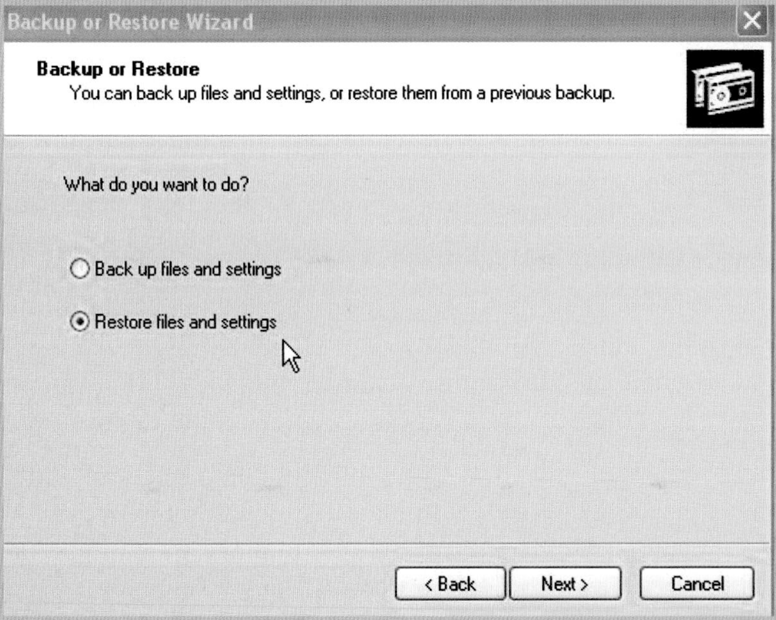

Figure 1.38: Restore files wizard.

▶ Click **Next**.

▶ Tick the backup you created in the previous activity from the list.

▶ Click **Next** to see a summary of your restore settings.

▶ Click **Finish** to start your restore.

▶ A **Restore Progress** information box will appear.

▶ Close the box when the restore is complete.

Key terms

Incremental (backup)

A backup in which only the changed data is backed up.

Portfolio builder

By working through Assessment Objective 1 you have learned how to create, edit and organise a computer filing system. Using the skills you have learned through the activities you should now be able to create a folder structure for your own portfolio. You may already know what the folder structure will be for your portfolio if you have agreed that with your teacher or tutor. However, in the event that you are not sure of the detail yet, you could make a start by creating a folder called OCR Nationals in ICT with six sub-folders, each called Assessment Objective 1, 2, etc. Remember, you may need more folders within each assessment objective. Make your tree structure as easy to understand as possible – this will help your teacher or tutor and moderator when they assess your portfolio.

Before you begin to collect evidence for your portfolio make sure you know which grade you are aiming for and then re-read the 'How to achieve' section at the beginning of each chapter so you know what you need to include in your portfolio for each assessment objective.

CHAPTER (2)

→ *Assessment Objective 2*
Searching the Internet and Using Email

. . . .

Overview:

In this chapter, you will learn how to search the World Wide Web effectively using appropriate software. You will learn how to evaluate the validity of the information that you download from the Internet and the implications of copyright. You will organise your work by learning how to use bookmarks and favourites.

You will also learn how to use emails appropriately and how to reduce the risks of receiving viruses via email attachments.

How this assessment objective will be assessed...

● You will need to produce screenshots for each task you undertake. Where you conduct a search, you will need to list some of the websites that you find. You will also need to save copies of emails.

● For a **Pass**, you will provide evidence of using search engines to find information. You will also provide evidence of sending, receiving, replying to and forwarding emails. Emails must include text and a header. You must provide evidence of your ability to send and receive an email attachment. Your explanation will comment on the risks of opening email attachments. For a **Merit,** you will show your understanding of the trustworthiness of different websites. You will also produce evidence of your use of bookmarks or favourites. Your notes will show that you understand copyright issues. For a **Distinction**, you will need to show an ability to use advanced search criteria. You will also comment on the validity of source material. You will organise your bookmarks/favourites into folders. You will show the ability to use address books, email signatures and attachments.

Skills to use...

You will need to:

● use search engines
● create and use bookmarks/favourites
● evaluate the validity of information on websites
● copy and paste text and graphics from websites
● download graphic and text files
● create, send, receive and forward emails and attachments
● create a signature
● assess the validity of emails and take action to avoid risks from receiving and opening attachments
● use cc and bcc
● use address books.

How to achieve...

Pass requirements

P1 You should use search engines to find information on the Internet and provide your source(s) website addresses.

P2 You should send, receive, reply and forward email, including at least one message with a document attached.

P3 You should open an attachment sent via email and save it to your work area.

P4 You should send messages to multiple recipients.

P5 You should comment about the risks of opening email attachments.

Merit requirements

M1 You should locate suitable elements from local media and the World Wide Web, using keywords.

M2 You should provide your source(s) website addresses and comment on the trustworthiness of your source.

M3 You should use bookmarks/favourites to store useful links.

M4 You should understand the implications of copyright.

M5 You should copy and paste text and graphics from the World Wide Web.

M6 You should send, receive, reply and forward email, including messages with multiple documents attached using appropriate subjects and message text.

M7 You should send messages to multiple recipients and understanding the use of cc.

M8 You should set messages as high or low importance.

M9 You should summarise the risks of receiving and opening email attachments.

Distinction requirements

D1 You should locate suitable elements from local media and the World Wide Web, making effective use of advanced search criteria.

D2 You should comment on the validity of your source(s).

D3 You should use bookmarks/favourites to store useful links and organise these into folders.

D4 You should understand the implications of copyright.

D5 You should download graphic and text files.

D6 You should acknowledge all sources used.

D7 You should send, receive, reply and forward email, including messages with multiple documents attached.

D8 You should send messages to multiple recipients using cc and bcc appropriately.

D9 You should store, retrieve and use email addresses and personal contacts details.

D10 You should make effective use of features of email software, including email signatures.

D11 You should consistently use appropriate subjects and message text.

D12 You should summarise the risks of receiving and opening email attachments and suggest actions that could be taken to reduce these risks.

An introduction to the Internet

Your school or college will probably have a set of computers networked together to form an Intranet. On a far larger scale, the Internet is a huge network of computers situated all around the world, which are connected together and exchange data using common software. Data is shared through telephone wires and satellite links. When your computer is connected to the Internet it can connect to millions of other computers worldwide.

The Internet allows you to:

- research information on any subject you can find
- chat to people all over the world
- play online games
- send and receive electronic mail (email)
- post information for others to access and update it frequently
- access **multimedia** information that includes sound, photographic images and even video
- buy things from a virtual shop and have goods delivered to your home
- check your bank details.

Key terms

Multimedia

The presentation of information by a computer system using graphics, animation, sound and text.

To view pages on the World Wide Web (WWW) you will need to use a program called a web browser. There are lots of different browsers; one of the most popular ones is Microsoft Internet Explorer.

Whichever web browser you use, you should be able to identify these features:

- a forward and back button

Figure 2.1: *Forward and back buttons.*

- an address box

http://www.google.co.uk/

Figure 2.2: *An address box.*

- a refresh button

Figure 2.3: *A refresh button.*

- a search box

Google

Figure 2.4: *A search box.*

● a favorites button

Figure 2.5: *A favorites button.*

A browser can be **configured** to include other features.

If you know the website address (URL) you can go to a particular page. The website address is made up of a number of parts, for example, look at **www.harcourt.co.uk**.

● **www** tells the computer that the information is on the World Wide Web.
● **harcourt** tells the computer to look for a file on the website of an organisation called Harcourt.
● **co.uk** tells the computer that the website belongs to a business in the United Kingdom.

You cannot include spaces in a website address; each part of the address is separated by a full stop. The names of other pages within the website are separated by a forward slash, for example, www.harcourt.co.uk/assets/about.html.

HTML (hypertext mark-up language) is the language used to create the web page. The file extension associated with html files is either .htm or .html.

Key terms

Configured

Configuration is an arrangement of features of the computer system or software.

Browsing the Internet

The Internet is vast – the more you visit it, the more comfortable you will become finding your way around it. The activity below shows you how to begin browsing.

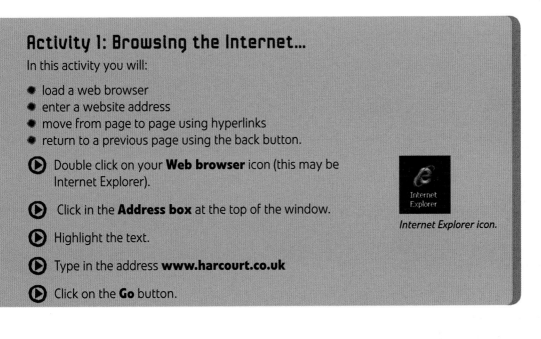

Activity 1: Browsing the Internet...

In this activity you will:

● load a web browser
● enter a website address
● move from page to page using hyperlinks
● return to a previous page using the back button.

▶ Double click on your **Web browser** icon (this may be Internet Explorer).

▶ Click in the **Address box** at the top of the window.

▶ Highlight the text.

▶ Type in the address **www.harcourt.co.uk**

▶ Click on the **Go** button.

Internet Explorer icon.

▶ Your screen should show the Harcourt home page.

Figure 2.6: *Harcourt's home page.*

Pages on the World Wide Web are linked so that you can move around them using hyperlinks. A hyperlink is a link in a web page to information somewhere else, either on the same website or on another website. A hyperlink can be an image or text.

▶ Move the mouse pointer over the **School Libraries** hotspot.

The cursor will change from an arrow to a hand.

Figure 2.7: *Hand pointer.*

> **⊙ TIP**
>
> A hyperlink is usually coloured in blue and underlined but it can also be an image. Some images used as hyperlinks can be called hotspots.

▶ Click on the hotspot – the browser will open a new web page.

▶ Click on the hyperlink **Big Books**.

▶ Your screen should look like the one in Figure 2.8.

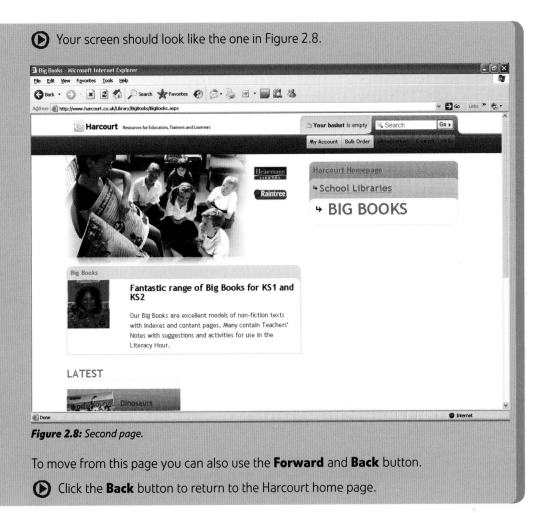

Figure 2.8: *Second page.*

To move from this page you can also use the **Forward** and **Back** button.

▶ Click the **Back** button to return to the Harcourt home page.

Search engines

There are billions of pages on the Web so it is important that you know how to search for what you need. Search engines are designed to help you find information quickly and efficiently.

Internet search engines are special websites (for example, Google and AltaVista) that help users find web pages on a given subject. The search engines keep databases of websites and use programs (often referred to as 'spiders' or 'robots') to collect information, which is then **indexed** by the search engine. Search engines and directories help you sift through all the information to find the specific information you need.

Search engines use software programs known as robots, spiders or crawlers. A robot is a piece of software that automatically follows hyperlinks from one document to the next around the Web. When a robot discovers a new site, it sends information back to its main site to be indexed. Because Web documents change a lot, robots also update previously catalogued sites.

Google, a popular search engine, is a tool for finding resources on the World Wide Web. Google scans web pages to find instances of the keywords you have entered in the search box.

> **⊙ TIP**
>
> Some search engines focus on particular types of information while others are more general. Choose a search engine that suits your needs.

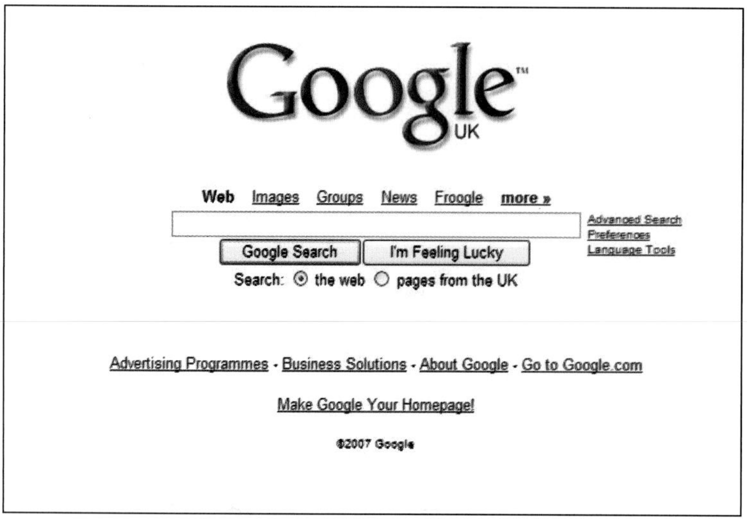

Figure 2.9: *Google.*

> ⊘ **TIP**
>
> The World Wide Web is like a huge library, containing lots of useful (and lots of not-so-useful) information. Remember, anyone can publish information on the Internet so not all the information you find will be accurate or reliable.

Keyword searching

A keyword in an Internet search is one of the words used to find matching web pages. A keyword can simply be any word on a web page but common words like 'a', 'and', 'or', 'but' are not treated as keywords because they are so common that it is inefficient to do so.

Many modern search engines can identify which words in a sentence are important and ought to be treated as keywords.

To search for a particular topic on the Internet, choose a search engine and type in your search criteria into the search box.

For example, to search for music, type in the keyword 'music' as shown in Figure 2.10:

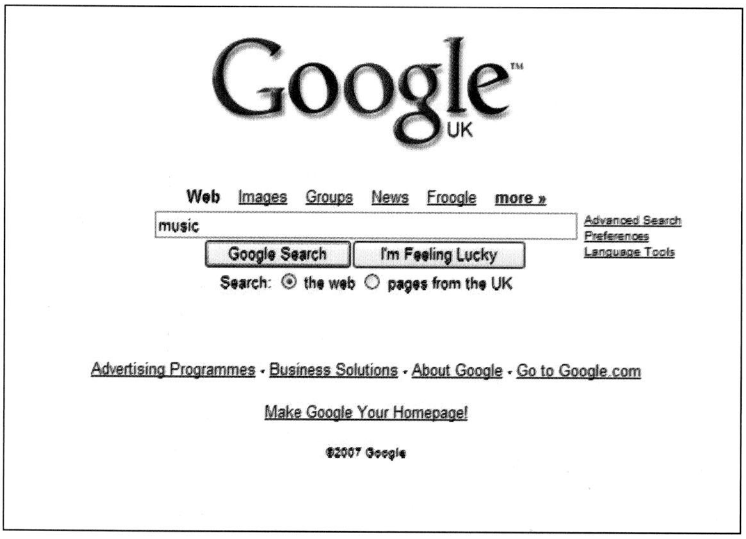

Figure 2.10: *A Google search.*

Most sites offer two different types of searches – 'basic' or 'advanced'. You will first carry out a basic, or simple, search.

Activity 2: Using a search engine...

In this activity you will:

● carry out a simple search to find information on the Internet.

▶ Load **Internet Explorer**.

▶ Enter www.google.co.uk into the **Address bar**.

▶ Click on the **Go** button.

▶ In the search box type **Belgian Sheepdog**.

You will see in the example below the top 10 references for pages containing the word Belgian and all the pages containing the word Sheepdog. The Web is always changing with new pages added and some removed so you are likely to get a different search result when you try this.

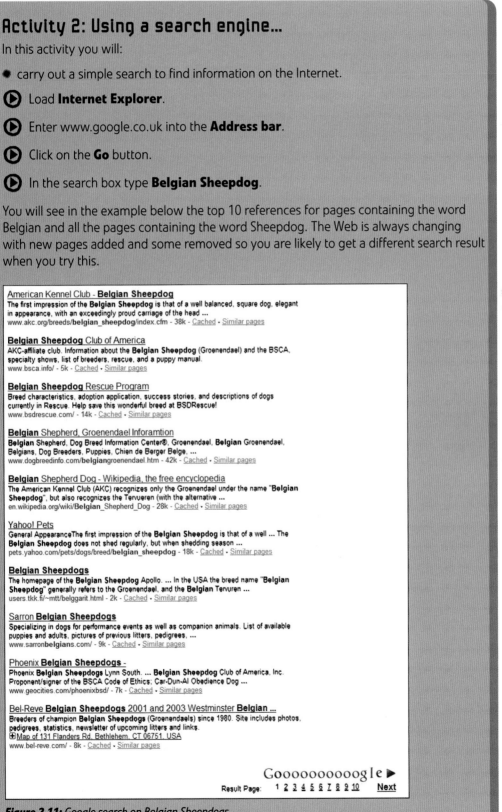

Figure 2.11: Google search on Belgian Sheepdogs.

Refining a search

You have probably noticed that simple searches produce too many results. There are times when you might need to use more complex searches to get more specific answers.

Activity 3: Refining your search...

In this activity you will:

- refine your search for Belgian Sheepdogs.

▶ Type **'Belgian Sheepdogs'** into the search box, including the quotation marks

This will search the whole phrase and will give far fewer results.

Many search engines allow you to use Boolean operators to refine your search. Below are some Boolean logical terms:

AND

This means that all the words in the search criteria must appear in the results i.e. 'big' AND 'dog'. You might use this if you wanted to exclude results that would be irrelevant to your search.

OR

This means that at least one of the words in your search criteria must appear in the results. You might use this if you didn't want to rule out too much.

NOT

This means that at least one of the words in your search criteria must NOT appear in the results.

> **①TIP**
>
> Use capitals when searching for proper names of people, companies or products. Unfortunately, many words in English are used as both proper and common nouns, for example, Bill, bill, Gates, gates and this will return unwanted results.

Using and organising bookmarks/favourites

As you use the Internet you will soon find websites that you want to revisit. Bookmarks and Favourites are two words for the same thing: they allow you to save Web addresses so you can return to them quickly, without having to retype them. Microsoft Internet Explorer uses the term 'favorite' (note the American spelling). Most other browsers use the term 'bookmark'.

Activity 4: Adding a page to the favourites list...

In this activity you will:

● add the location of a web page to your favourites folder.

▶ Open a web page.

▶ Click the **Favorites** button on the toolbar. The favourites panel will appear to the left of the browser window.

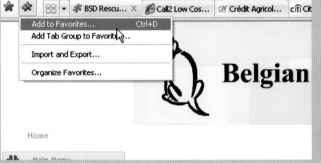

Figure 2.12: Favorites.

▶ Click the **Add** button. The **Add Favorite** dialogue box will appear.

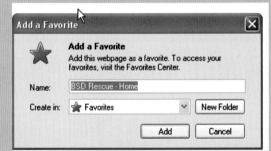

Figure 2.13: Add a Favorite.

▶ Click **OK** if you are happy with the suggested name or type a new name in the **Name box**.

The web page address will now be included in your list of favourites.

▶ Double click on the name to access the page again

As your bookmark/favourites collection grows you should sort them into categories and folders to make them easier to find.

In Chapter 1 we looked at organising files and folders so that you can find your work easily at a later date. This rule applies not only to your desktop files but also to your favourites list. Once you have collected a number of favourites links, you can organise them into folders.

You will need to give the folders meaningful names so that you can just click the folder and see a list of all your favourites in that group. For example, you might create a folder called favourite music links and another folder for links to your favourite radio station websites.

Activity 5: Organising your favourites into folders...

In this activity you will:

● organise favourites into folders
● give a folder a meaningful name.

▶ In **Internet Explorer**, click the **Add to Favorites** button.

▶ Click **Organize Favorites**.

Figure 2.14: *Organize Favorites.*

▶ In the **Organize Favorites** dialog box, click **New Folder**.

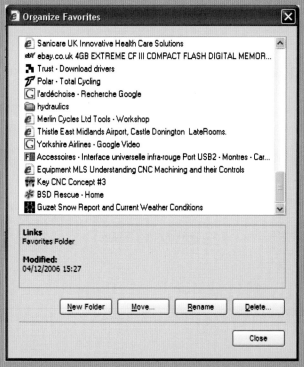

Figure 2.15: *New folder.*

▶ Type a meaningful name for the folder.

▶ Press **Enter**.

▶ Drag favourites from the list into the appropriate new folder.

▶ Click **Done**.

Evaluating the validity of information

The World Wide Web provides information and data from all over the world. When you use paper based resources for research they have already been evaluated by publishers. However, when you are using the World Wide Web, none of this applies; anyone can publish information on any subject they wish – you do not have to be an expert or famous author. Much of the information is produced by unknown people. This means that there is a wide range in the quality and accuracy of the information available.

For example, how do you know if a website giving legal information has been written by a trained lawyer or just a clever 16-year-old? How old is the information; is it up to date? How do you know if you can trust the information given?

It is important to be sure that the information you have is reliable and accurate and so you need to develop skills to evaluate what you find for yourself. You should always list the address of any websites from which you have sourced information.

Checking the validity of information on a website

When checking the validity of information you find on a website, there are a number of questions you should ask yourself:

● Who wrote the page and can you contact him or her?

Examine the URL – look for a personal name (for example, *nwilliams* or *nwilliams*) following a tilde (~) or a per cent sign (%).

If the URL is from a personal page, it may only reflect an individual's views.

● Is this person qualified to write this document?

Personal pages are not necessarily 'bad' but you need to investigate the author very carefully. An email address alone is not enough information to verify the author's identity.

● Where is the document published?

Check the URL domain (educational, non-profit, commercial, government, etc). Domains include:

- o com – a **commercial site**. They might be trying to sell you something so they might not be very objective.
- o edu – an **academic site**. Check the credibility of the author. Look for an 'about the author' link.
- o gov – a reliable source but it may be biased towards the Government's point of view.
- o org – used by non-profit groups such as charities and religious groups. These sites may be biased towards the organisation's point of view.

Key terms

Commercial site

A business website that trades goods or services for profit.

Academic site

A website that focuses on educational information.

Copying and pasting text and graphics from the Web

The Web can be an excellent source of text and graphics that you can reproduce in your own work. However, before you copy and paste, you need to make sure that you are not infringing (breaking) any copyright laws.

Copyright

Information on the World Wide Web is protected by copyright laws. While it is readily available and usually free of charge, if you copy it without permission, you could be breaking copyright laws.

The Copyright, Designs and Patents Act, 1988 makes it illegal to copy text or images or logos from the Internet and then re-use them without permission from the copyright owner.

Some websites give permission for their material to be used for educational or non-profit making purposes. You should look for a statement of permission, which is usually on the home page of the site.

Before you use content from another website you should contact the author of the material to ask for permission. This may not always be successful.

Even when the site supplying the material declares that material is copyright free, the site itself may not be the ultimate copyright holder.

Copying from web pages

Copy and **Paste** are computer functions that allow you to move information from one place to another without deleting it from the original location.

The copy function stores information in the computer's memory in an area called the **Clipboard** (the temporary storage area in a computer's memory). Some of the latest word processing applications allow you to keep more than one item on the clipboard.

It is possible to copy text and images from a website into another document stored on your computer.

Activity 6: Copying text and graphics from a web page...

In this activity you will:

- copy and paste text from a web page
- copy and paste an image from a web page.

▶ Open a web browser and go to the page with the text you want to copy.

▶ On the web page, highlight the text you want to copy.

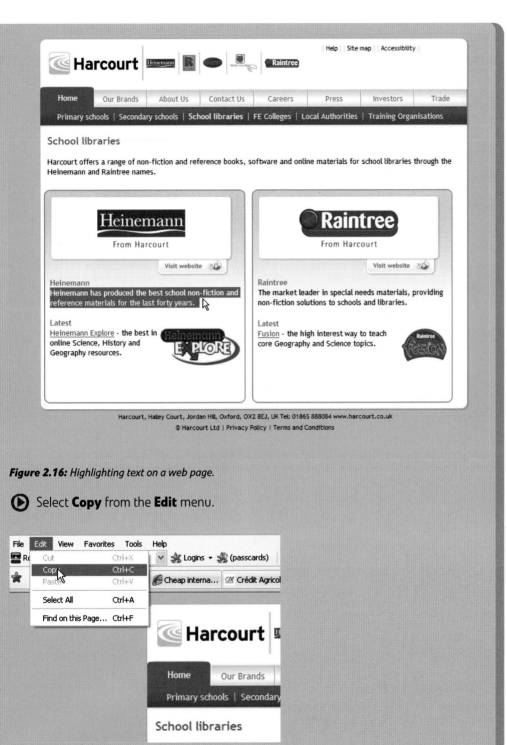

Figure 2.16: *Highlighting text on a web page.*

▶ Select **Copy** from the **Edit** menu.

Figure 2.17: *Copy text.*

▶ Open a word processing document.

▶ Right click where you want the text to appear.

▶ Save your document.

To copy and paste an entire web page into a word document:

- ▶ Click your mouse anywhere in the document or web page.

- ▶ Go to the **Edit** menu.

- ▶ Choose **Select All** to automatically highlight all the text and images on the page.

- ▶ From the **Edit** menu select **Copy**.

- ▶ Open a word document.

- ▶ From the **Edit** menu select **Paste**.

To copy and paste an image from a web page:

- ▶ In **Internet Explorer**, browse to a web page with a picture you want to save.

- ▶ Right click the picture and select **Copy**.

- ▶ Paste it into your word document.

If you want to save the file for use later:

- ▶ Right click the picture and select **Copy**.

- ▶ Click **Save Picture As**.

- ▶ In the **Save Picture** dialog box, browse to the folder where you want to save the file and then click **Save**.

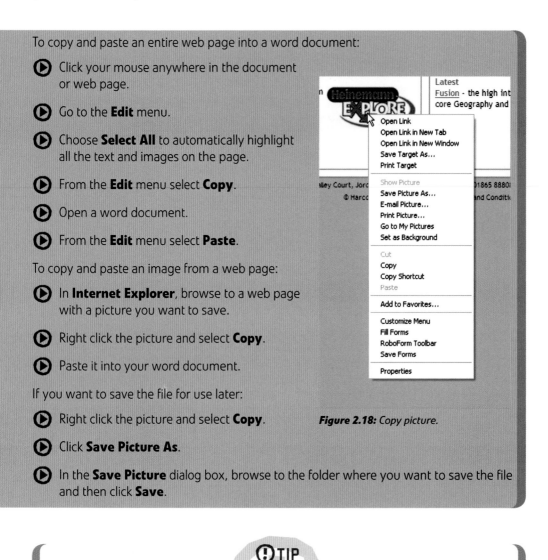

Figure 2.18: Copy picture.

> **① TIP**
>
> If you use the Save As option, give your file a meaningful name and store it in a place where you will find it easily in the future, with the rest of your graphics files.

Downloading files

It is possible to download many different types of files from the Internet including video clips and software, etc. As you will probably download a large number of files from the Internet, it is important that you keep a record of where you found your information, as you may need to acknowledge its source at a later date. You should also keep a record of the name and address of the site and the date the site was used, as well as the date that the site was last updated.

Email – an important form of communication

When computers are networked, you can send electronic mail (email) from one computer to another.

Like a letter, an email is a permanent record of a message and the person receiving the email can choose whether or not to read it. Unlike a letter, which has to be delivered manually using the postal system, email can be delivered almost immediately anywhere in the world.

Email has become very popular as a means of communication with people all over the world because it is fast and convenient. Despite the distance between the sender and the receiver, an email message can find its way anywhere in the world within seconds or minutes. Many people now use email as a communication method as part of their working and personal life.

An email message is simply an electronic note sent between computer users over the Internet or some other computer network. Emails can simply be text or they can include attached files, for example, a word processed document or an image file.

To send and receive emails you need an email address and a program to send and receive emails (usually called an email client).

The email can be written off-line, using an email program or software. The user then connects online to an **Internet Service Provider** (ISP) to send the email. For some types of email services, like Hotmail, you need to be online to compose the email. This sort of email is often called webmail.

Key terms

Internet Service Provider

An organisation which offers computer users access to the Internet, email and websites.

When email is received on a computer system, it is usually stored in your own personal electronic mailbox.

Emails are made up of two parts: the header and the body.

- **The header** – the message header consists of fields, usually including at least the following:

  From: The email address of the sender of the message
  To: The email address(es) of the receiver(s) of the message
  Subject: A brief summary of the contents of the message
  Date: The local time and date when the message was originally sent

  The headers can also be extended to show more detailed information.

- **The body** – this is the actual content of the email message.

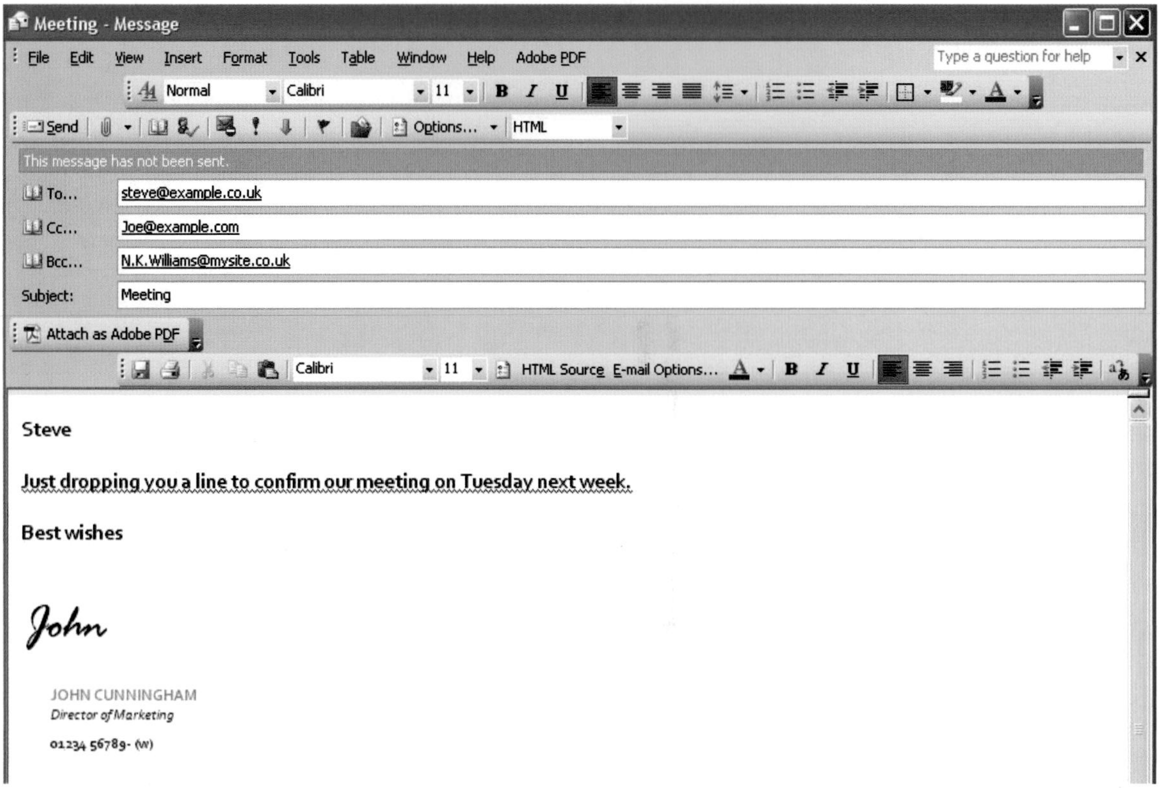

Figure 2.19: *An email.*

Composing emails

When you are writing your emails, there are some essential items that you must include. These are:

- the address of the recipient
- the address(es) of anyone that should receive a copy of your email
- the subject of your email
- your message.

The email address

Just like a letter, you need to make sure that you have the correct address for the recipient so that it will be delivered to the right place.

Email addresses usually follow a standard format, starting with the email name of the person, followed by various address components, ending in the country code (just like a conventional letter). For example: N.K.Williams@mysite.co.uk

Figure 2.20: *An email address.*

The email name comes first, indicating who the email is for. The @ sign separates the email name from the site.

The next components, separated by full stops, tell you more details about where the email has come from.

!TIP

With email you need to be even more precise and accurate than when addressing a conventional letter.

Cc and Bcc

Cc stands for carbon copy or courtesy copy. Everyone in this box will receive an exact copy of the email.

Bcc stands for blind carbon copy. This is the same as **Cc**, except that the list of people who will receive a copy of the email are not shown. This is particularly useful if you want to send an email to many people but you don't want them to see each other's email addresses or to know who else has received a copy of the message.

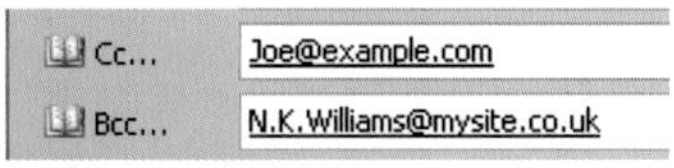

Cc...	Joe@example.com
Bcc...	N.K.Williams@mysite.co.uk

Figure 2.21: *Cc and Bcc.*

The title of the email or subject line

The subject of an email is important as it gives the person receiving the message key information about its content. Always include a subject line in your message. Make sure it is meaningful and descriptive (for example, 'IT book – first draft', not 'Hi'). If a subject is not included in an email many spam filters consider it 'junk-mail' and will deal with it accordingly.

!TIP

Always include a subject title for your email. Messages with subject lines are more likely to be read!

Subject:	Meeting

Figure 2.22: *The subject line.*

The email body

This is where you type the email message.

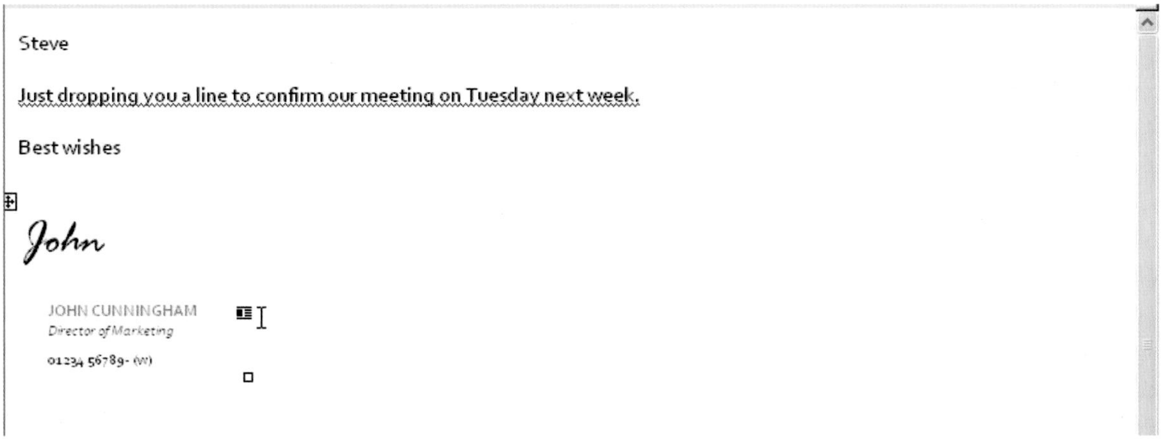

Steve

Just dropping you a line to confirm our meeting on Tuesday next week.

Best wishes

John

JOHN CUNNINGHAM
Director of Marketing
01234 56789- (w)

Figure 2.23: *Email body.*

Sending emails and setting importance

Activity 7: Sending emails...

In this activity you will:

- send an email message to one or more recipients
- set an email as high or low importance.

▶ Open your email program.

▶ On the **File** menu, click **New**.

▶ Click **Mail Message**.

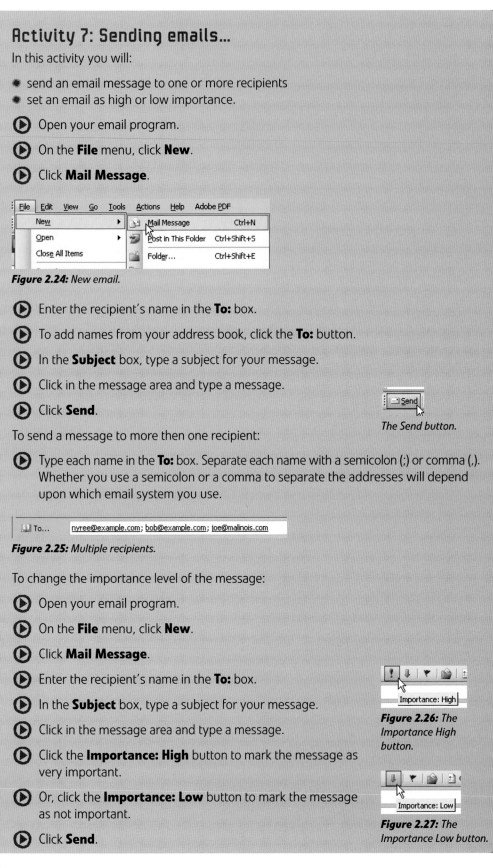

Figure 2.24: New email.

▶ Enter the recipient's name in the **To:** box.

▶ To add names from your address book, click the **To:** button.

▶ In the **Subject** box, type a subject for your message.

▶ Click in the message area and type a message.

▶ Click **Send**.

The Send button.

To send a message to more then one recipient:

▶ Type each name in the **To:** box. Separate each name with a semicolon (;) or comma (,). Whether you use a semicolon or a comma to separate the addresses will depend upon which email system you use.

To...   nyree@example.com; bob@example.com; joe@malinois.com

Figure 2.25: Multiple recipients.

To change the importance level of the message:

▶ Open your email program.

▶ On the **File** menu, click **New**.

▶ Click **Mail Message**.

▶ Enter the recipient's name in the **To:** box.

▶ In the **Subject** box, type a subject for your message.

▶ Click in the message area and type a message.

▶ Click the **Importance: High** button to mark the message as very important.

Figure 2.26: The Importance High button.

▶ Or, click the **Importance: Low** button to mark the message as not important.

▶ Click **Send**.

Figure 2.27: The Importance Low button.

Formatting tools

These tools allow you to change the size, colour and layout, etc., of your text, just like using a word processor.

Figure 2.28: *The email formatting toolbar.*

Using email with caution

Emails are very quick and easy to write so you need to be careful about what you send. Anyone can easily forward your message, even accidentally. This could leave you in an embarrassing position if you include personal or confidential (private) information.

Just like writing a letter or making a telephone call there are certain rules (sometimes called email etiquette) that you should follow:

- Never send confidential information such as bank details in an email as these could be read by other people.
- Try to avoid sending attachments unless it is necessary as wireless devices and mobile phones may not have the software needed to open the attachment.
- Always read your email (and attachments) to check for errors before sending.

Emoticons (or smileys) should only be used in informal emails to friends and family. They are not appropriate for formal emails. Avoid the use of abbreviations such as BTW (by the way) and LOL (laugh out loud). The recipient might not understand the abbreviations and in formal emails these are not appropriate.

Check who your message is going to. If the mail that you are replying to was addressed to several people, clicking on the 'reply' button may send your response to everyone in the address bar. This can be very annoying or embarrassing if your reply was only intended for one person.

Using appropriate language in emails

Try not to use capital letters as it makes your message more difficult to read. It also makes it look as if you are shouting!

Use proper spelling, grammar and punctuation to avoid confusion in your email messages. Emails with no full stops or commas are difficult to read and can sometimes even change the meaning of the text.

Keep your messages short and focused. People tend to ignore long messages. The person receiving your email may be reading it on a mobile phone or small screen and may not be able to read a long message.

> **⊙TIP**
> Use the email software spell checker to check your spelling before sending the email.

Email signatures

A 'signature' is a small block of text which can be added to the end of each message you send. Signatures usually contain your contact information and help the person reading the email to identify you.

TIP

Keep your signature short and precise.

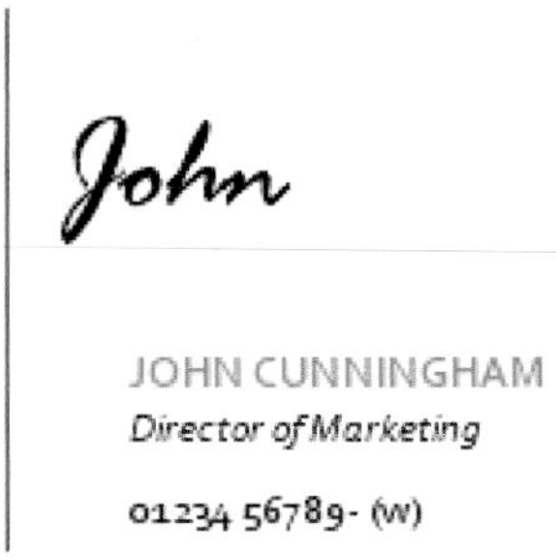
John
JOHN CUNNINGHAM
Director of Marketing
01234 56789- (w)

Figure 2.29: *An email signature.*

Activity 8: Creating an email signature

In this activity you will:

- Create a signature to add to an email message

- In the e-mail message, on the **Tools** menu, click **Options**, and then click the **General** tab.
- Click **E-mail Options**, and then click the **E-mail Signature** tab.
- In the **Type the title of your e-mail signature or choose from the list** box, click the name of the e-mail signature you want to use.
- Under **Create your e-mail signature**, select the signature text you want to add to your e-mail message and then press CTRL+C.
- Click **Close**, and then click **Cancel**.
- In the e-mail message, place your cursor where you want the signature to appear, and then press CTRL+V.

There are lots of other ways to communicate using the Internet besides email and the list is growing all the time. Some examples are instant messaging, **blogging**, text messaging, chat, **Skype**, etc.

Key terms

Blogging

A blog is a personal journal-style website and blogging is the process of adding comments to a particular topic.

Skype

An Internet-based telephone communication system.

Email attachments and risks

Attachments are files that are included in an email message that is to be sent. They increase the size of the email and large attachments can be slow to send.

Most attachments are completely legitimate, for example, family photos or homework files. However, viruses are sometimes sent via attachments to emails. These attachments can be disguised to trick you into opening them. Some attachments are embedded in emails that look like web pages. Even opening these types of email can infect your computer with spy ware or viruses.

> ⊘ **TIP**
> Compress the attachment to make it as small as possible.

To reduce the risk of opening email attachments with viruses you should:

- use anti-virus software
- set your email client to open emails in text-only mode
- set security controls to warn you when you open any email attachment
- use spam and junk mail functions to stop unwanted emails.

Not all attachments can be opened and read by the person to whom you are sending the files. Make sure that they have the correct software installed on their computer before you send an attachment. Instead of sending an attachment, consider putting the text you wish to send in the body of your email or send an URL (web address) or some other reference instead.

Attachments can contain viruses. Many viruses have been spread by using email attachments and for security reasons many receiving email systems can block or return them. Only open an attachment if you are sure that you can trust the sender.

> **TIP**
> When sending an attachment via email, it's always a good idea to mention that you've attached a file in case your recipient's mail program loses it (or you have forgotten to attach it).

Activity 9: Sending and receiving attachments...

In this activity you will:

- send an email with one or more attachments
- save an attachment

To attach a file to an email:

▶ Click the **Insert File** button.

The **Insert File** box will appear.

The Insert File button.

Figure 2.30: The Insert File box.

▶ Choose a file to add to your email.

▶ Click **Insert**.

The attachment name will appear in the **Attach:** box.

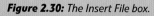

Figure 2.31: The Attach box.

The message now has an attachment. You can add further attachments by repeating the process above for each attachment.

You will need to add a subject, recipients and the message before sending.

To download an attachment from an email you have received:

▶ Highlight the attachment name by clicking once.

▶ Right click on the name of the attachment.

▶ Select **Save As**.

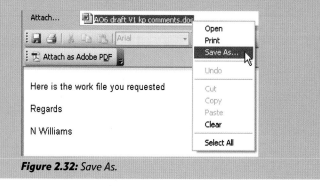

Figure 2.32: Save As.

The **Save Attachment** box will appear.

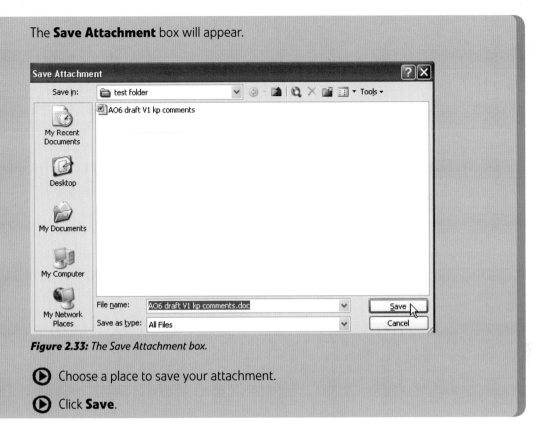

Figure 2.33: *The Save Attachment box.*

▶ Choose a place to save your attachment.

▶ Click **Save**.

Activity 10: How to forward and reply to emails...

In this activity you will:

● Reply to an email message

▶ Open an email message in your **Inbox**.

▶ Click the **Reply** button on the toolbar. A new message window will appear.

The Reply button.

The email address of the sender will automatically be displayed in the **To:** box.

Re: will automatically be added to the beginning of the subject.

▶ Type a reply to the message in the message area.

▶ Press **Enter** to insert a line after your message.

▶ Type your name.

▶ Click the **Send** button on the toolbar.

⋮ ▭ Send ⃒

The Send button.

▶ The message will be sent and the **New Message** window will close.

To forward an email:

▶ Open an email message in your **Inbox**.

▶ Click the **Forward** button on the toolbar.

Forward

The Forward button.

A new message window will open. The **To:** box will be empty, the **Subject:** box will show the same subject as the original message.

▶ Click in the **To:** box and type the email address given by your tutor.

▶ Click in the message area and type a message.

▶ Press **Enter** to insert a line after your message.

▶ Type your name.

▶ Click the **Send** button on the toolbar.

▶ The message will be sent and the **New Message** window will close.

The validity of emails

You might have received emails that appear to be from one source but are actually from somewhere else. False emails are often a way of trying to trick people into giving out personal information such as passwords or bank details. It is important that you can recognise these emails so that you do not get caught out.

You may receive a very official looking email that appears to come from a genuine online bank or online payment service. Those that have been used include PayPal, eBay, MSN, Yahoo, Barclays Bank and Lloyds TSB. This type of email attempts to collect personal and financial information from you.

The message might say that there is something wrong with your account and that you need to re-enter your registration or account information, or it might ask you to re-activate your account. There may be a threat that you will lose your account if you do not respond immediately.

You may be asked to click on a link to log in and begin using your updated account. Many false emails include links to web pages and these can be forged too. Forged links will take you to a fake website. Often the link in the email will not match the URL of the site it takes you to.

False emails can look remarkably like the real ones. Requests that you enter sensitive information are a clear indicator of a trick. Companies will not ask you to send passwords or personal details so you should never reply to these emails.

The 'From' field of an email can be easily altered to any name so it is not a reliable indicator of the sender's true identity. **Spoof email** may include a forged email address in the 'From' line.

Key terms

Spoof email

A term used to describe forged or false emails aimed at misleading the recipient.

!TIP

Only click on a link in an email if you are certain of the source of the email.

The email address book

An address book is the place where you store all your email addresses and other contact details. Each entry about a person is called a contact. You can add to and change the information you have about each of your contacts. Address books can contain as little or as much information as you wish. For example, your personal contacts might include details such as birthdays, nicknames, addresses and telephone numbers. Contacts can be stored as individuals and/or groups. You can set your email to add each new address to your address book automatically.

The address book is useful for sorting and retrieving contact details, especially if you have a large number of contacts to search. With electronic address books you can search your contacts using different criteria, which is useful as often the email address is very different to someone's name.

!TIP

Remember to back up your address book regularly to avoid losing all your contact details.

Portfolio evidence

Based on the topic area that you have chosen in conjunction with your teacher or tutor, use the 'How to achieve' section at the beginning of this chapter to guide you in searching the Internet and using email at the level towards which you are working.

The previous sections have given you some indication of how you could go about browsing the Internet and sending and receiving emails. You should think about:

- the validity of any information you find on the Internet
- the copyright implications of any information you download
- how effectively you use bookmarks and favourites
- the appropriate use of emails
- taking steps to protect against viruses sent via email attachments
- using screenshots to provide proof of your work.

CHAPTER ③

→ *Assessment Objective 3*

Producing a Business Presentation Using Presentation Software

Overview:

In this chapter, you will produce a business presentation using presentation software. You will use existing templates to produce screen layouts. You will learn how to create and position text and graphic frames and how to improve your presentation by editing screen and content layout and by applying slide transition effects. You will check your presentation for errors.

You will also learn how to add speaker notes and print out your slides in handout form with speaker notes.

In order to complete the activities in this chapter you will need access to an additional file. This file is contained in the Chapter 3 Resources zip file which can be downloaded from the OCR Nationals in ICT (Units 1 and 21) Student Resources page on the Payne-Gallway website: www.payne-gallway.co.uk.

* **Axel and Buster.jpg**

How this assessment objective will be assessed...

* You will need to produce a presentation. You should save copies of your presentation as it develops.
* You need to provide sufficient evidence of your presentation you have created, for example:
    * printout(s) of the presentation
    * screenshot(s) of techniques used to create the presentation
    * witness statements to show the appropriateness of the presentation for the intended audience.

Skills to use...

You will need to:

* use text and graphic frames
* use slide transitions and screen layouts
* use software to edit screen content and layout
* create speaker notes
* carry out error and style checks
* print out slides.

How to achieve...

Pass requirements

P1 You should produce a business presentation of at least three slides using text and graphics.

P2 You should check the presentation for errors.

Merit requirements

M1 You should produce a business presentation of at least four slides using appropriate text and graphics.

M2 You should use a consistent style.

M3 You should set slide transitions.

M4 You should check the presentation is free from obvious errors.

M5 You should print out the presentation in handout form.

Distinction requirements

D1 You should produce a business presentation of at least five slides using appropriate text and graphics.

D2 You should set slide transitions and animation.

D3 You should check the presentation to ensure it is appropriate for the purpose and audience.

D4 You should add speaker notes where appropriate.

D5 You should print out the presentation in handout form, showing the notes pages.

Business presentations

Businesses often need to present information to an audience, for example, updating employees on the company's performance or presenting new ideas to a Senior Management Team, either within or external to their company, for approval. You are probably used to your teacher or tutor presenting new information to you via a presentation on the whiteboard. The purpose of a presentation is often to get the main points of information across to an audience who know nothing, or very little, about what you are presenting. So you need to choose your information, and the way that you put it across, very carefully to ensure that the audience comes away with a clear understanding of the issues you are presenting.

Presentation software is usually used for this as it is easy to combine text, graphics, animations and sound files, video clips and Internet pages, making the presentation as interesting and informative as possible for the audience. The information is presented as a series of slides which complement input from the speaker. The slides should only include the main points around which the presenter is talking – they should not include everything the presenter says.

The presentation is usually made via a computer screen or using a projector onto a whiteboard.

There are many different presentation software packages available but you are probably most familiar with Microsoft PowerPoint. Activity 1 leads you through the steps of how to create your own presentation. Before you start, however, there are a number of things that you should consider as part of your planning.

Planning your presentation

Here are a few guidelines to follow when planning a presentation:

- Keep the information simple and only include essential information.
- Try not to put too much information on each slide – use a few bullet points to highlight key points.
- Avoid using too many slides.
- Keep to a logical order and layout.
- Avoid using CAPITAL LETTERS.
- Keep fonts simple, limit the number of fonts you include and make sure that the font size is big enough for the presentation to be seen from a distance.
- Keep the background simple so that it doesn't distract from the content of the slides.
- Don't overuse slide animations and transitions as this can become annoying for the audience.
- Make your presentation interesting by combining text with images.

A new presentation

You may not know much about Belgian Sheepdogs, but if the presentation you create in the activities below follows the rules above, you should, by the end of the five slides, be able to remember the basic facts about them.

Activity 1: Creating a new presentation...

In this activity you will:

- create a new presentation and add new slides with tables.

▶ Open the **PowerPoint** program.

▶ Click **Blank presentation** – the slide layout options should appear.

▶ Select **Title** and **Text** in the **Text Layouts** box.

Figure 3.1: *Selecting a blank presentation.*

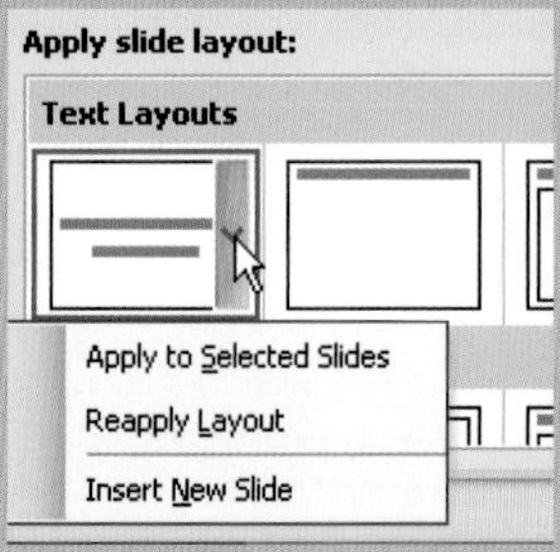

Figure 3.2: *Text Layout option.*

▶ Type the title **Dog Breeds** into the title box.

▶ Add the subtitle **The Belgian Sheepdog** into the subtitle box.

▶ Save your presentation with the name **Belgian Sheepdogs**.

Figure 3.3: Saving your file.

Now you are going to add new slides to your presentation.

▶ Click the **New Slide** icon on the toolbar – the default layout should be **Title and Text**.

The New Slide icon.

▶ Type in the text shown in Figure 3.4.

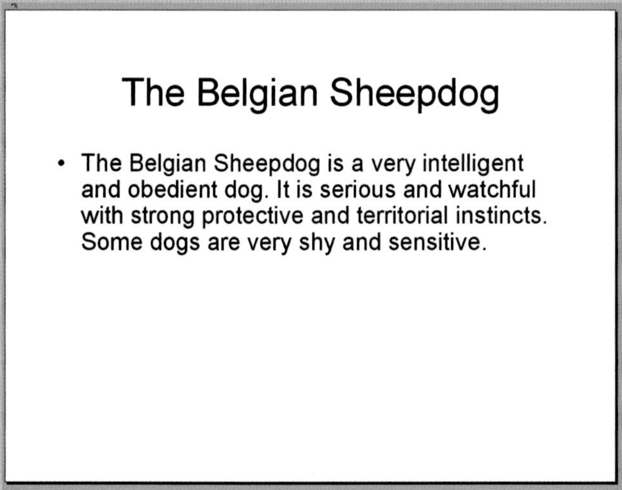

The Belgian Sheepdog

- The Belgian Sheepdog is a very intelligent and obedient dog. It is serious and watchful with strong protective and territorial instincts. Some dogs are very shy and sensitive.

Figure 3.4: Text for your new slide.

▶ Now click the New Slide icon again to create a new slide with the text shown in Figure 3.5.

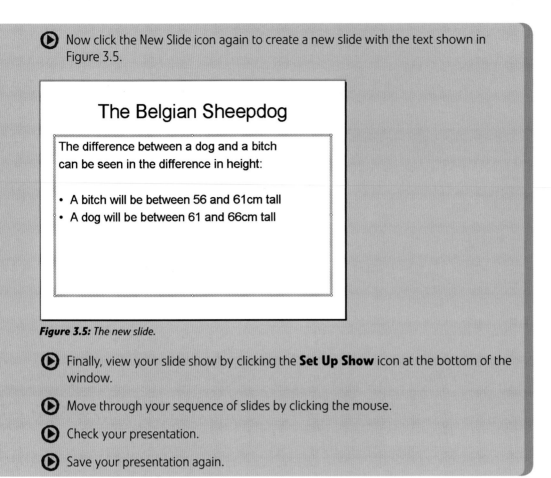

The Belgian Sheepdog

The difference between a dog and a bitch can be seen in the difference in height:

- A bitch will be between 56 and 61cm tall
- A dog will be between 61 and 66cm tall

Figure 3.5: *The new slide.*

▶ Finally, view your slide show by clicking the **Set Up Show** icon at the bottom of the window.

▶ Move through your sequence of slides by clicking the mouse.

▶ Check your presentation.

▶ Save your presentation again.

Adding images

To make your business presentation successful you need to keep your audience interested so the next activity is about adding a **visual element** to your presentation.

Key terms

Visual element

A chart, diagram, image or video clip, other than text which is added to enhance a presentation.

Activity 2: Adding and formatting an image...

In this activity you will:

- add a title and image to a slide
- reposition an image.

▶ Open the PowerPoint presentation called **Belgian Sheepdogs**.

▶ Create a new slide with the **Title and Text** layout.

▶ Type the title **The Belgian Sheepdog** in the title box.

Now you are going to add an image into the box below.

▶ Delete the text and bullet point in the text box.

▶ Click **Insert** on the menu bar, and then select **Picture, From File**. The **Insert Picture** dialogue box appears.

The Set Up Show icon.

Figure 3.6: *Adding an image.*

▶ Find the file called **Axel and Buster.jpg**. You should have downloaded this graphic file at the beginning of this unit.

▶ Select the file **Axel and Buster.jpg** and then click **Insert**.

Now you are going to reposition the image so that it is central to the frame. The easiest way to move images is by dragging them to their new position.

▶ Click once on the image to reveal the handles.

Figure 3.7: *Picture handles.*

(▶) Make sure the mouse pointer has changed to a cross.

(▶) Drag the cross and use the handles until the picture is in the correct position and is the correct size as shown below.

(▶) Save your presentation.

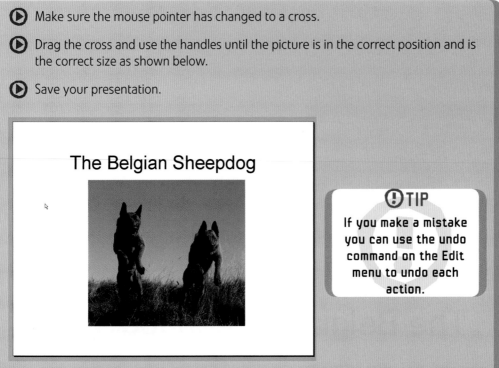

Figure 3.8: *The picture inserted.*

Slide transitions

Another way of adding interest to your presentation is by including movement (**transition**) in your slides.

Key terms

Transition

Different effects that can be used when changing from one slide to another.

Activity 3: Adding slide transitions and animations...

In this activity you will:

- apply a slide transition
- animate text.

(▶) Open the **PowerPoint** program.

(▶) Open the presentation called **Belgian Sheepdogs**.

(▶) Right click the thumbnail image of slide 2.

(▶) Select **Slide Transition**.

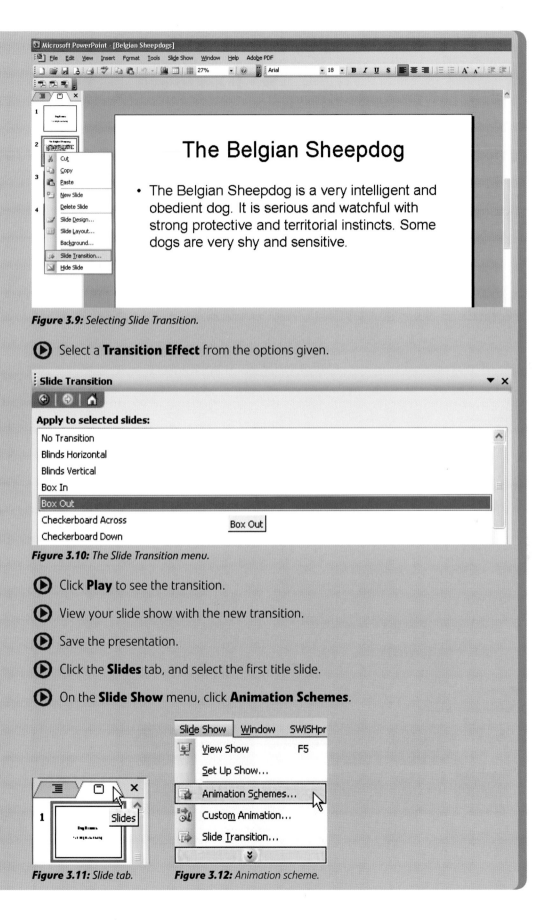

Figure 3.9: *Selecting Slide Transition.*

▶ Select a **Transition Effect** from the options given.

Figure 3.10: *The Slide Transition menu.*

▶ Click **Play** to see the transition.

▶ View your slide show with the new transition.

▶ Save the presentation.

▶ Click the **Slides** tab, and select the first title slide.

▶ On the **Slide Show** menu, click **Animation Schemes**.

Figure 3.11: *Slide tab.*   **Figure 3.12:** *Animation scheme.*

> **TIP**
>
> Run through your presentation beforehand to check the timing and decide how long each slide is viewed. You can do this by using the **Advance slide** section of the **Slide Transition** menu.

Using templates

Templates are a very useful tool as they set standards for a presentation, such as the background, font type, size and colour and these give a consistency to the whole presentation.

Using a template also means that you can make changes to the template which affect the entire presentation rather than having to change each individual slide.

> **TIP**
>
> Microsoft PowerPoint includes two types of template to help you build your presentations: design templates and content templates.

Key terms

Templates

A pre-developed layout used to create new documents or files from the same design, pattern, or style.

Activity 4: Creating a presentation using an existing template...

In this activity you will:

- use an existing template to create a presentation.

▶ Open the **PowerPoint** program.

▶ Open the presentation called **Belgian Sheepdogs**.

▶ Select a design from the **Design template** options.

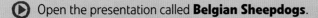

The Slide Design icon.

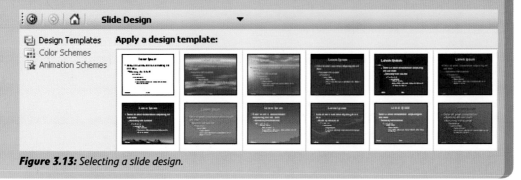

Figure 3.13: *Selecting a slide design.*

▶ Select by clicking on your chosen design.

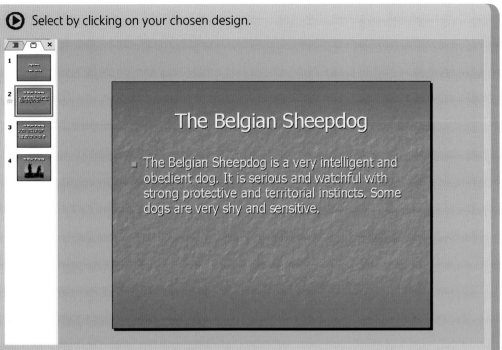

Figure 3.14: *Selecting a design for your presentation.*

Reordering and editing the slides

Having creating your slides you will need make sure that they are in a logical order that gives a clear message to your audience. Presentation applications make it easy to edit your slides. You can add slides, modify content, change the order or remove slides completely.

Activity 5: Reordering and editing slides...

In this activity you will:

● reorder the slides in your presentation
● edit the content of the slides in your presentation.

▶ Open the PowerPoint presentation called **Belgian Sheepdogs**.

▶ You are going to use the **Slide Sorter View** to reorder the slides.

▶ Click the **Slide Sorter View** icon on the bottom of the screen. You should see all the slides as a series of numbered thumbnail images.

The Slide Sorter View icon.

▶ Click on **Slide 4** and hold down the left mouse button.

▶ Drag the slide to the right so that the vertical line appears after **Slide 1**.

▶ Release the mouse button and your slides should now be in their new order.

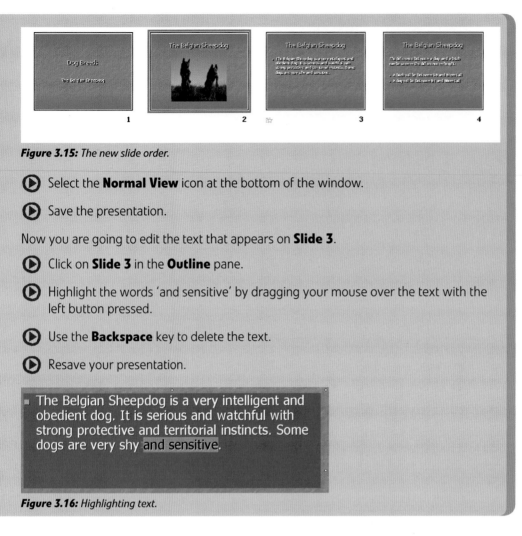

Figure 3.15: *The new slide order.*

▶ Select the **Normal View** icon at the bottom of the window.

▶ Save the presentation.

Now you are going to edit the text that appears on **Slide 3**.

▶ Click on **Slide 3** in the **Outline** pane.

▶ Highlight the words 'and sensitive' by dragging your mouse over the text with the left button pressed.

▶ Use the **Backspace** key to delete the text.

▶ Resave your presentation.

> ▪ The Belgian Sheepdog is a very intelligent and obedient dog. It is serious and watchful with strong protective and territorial instincts. Some dogs are very shy and sensitive.

Figure 3.16: *Highlighting text.*

Types of view

Most presentation software has different views to help you see your work as it develops. There are three main types of view: normal view, slide sorter view and slide show view. You can select one of these to be your default view.

● **Normal**
The text outline of the entire presentation is on the left, the current slide is on the upper-right and the speaker notes are on the lower-right.

● **Slide sorter**
This view shows the entire set of slides (numbered) on the screen. It allows you to drag-and-drop slide icons to change their order.

● **Slide show**
This view displays the presentation in full-screen mode starting with the slide that was last edited.

There are other views that you may also find useful when developing your presentation:

- **Outline**
  This view provides a large text outline area.
- **Slide**
  This shows a graphic view of the current slide.
- **Notes page**
  This lets you view the speaker notes on a slide.

Creating speaker notes

At the beginning we said that the slides used in a presentation should not include everything that a presenter says. This means that a presenter often needs notes to remind them what they are going to say in their presentation based around their slides. PowerPoint has a facility for adding speaker notes to a presentation. As well as helping you to remember key points during a presentation, they can also be used for printed handouts which you can give to your audience after you have completed your presentation.

You can print out the notes for each slide, along with a smaller version of the slide, as a reminder of the content of the presentation.

Activity 6: Adding speaker notes...

In this activity you will:

- add speaker notes to the presentation.

▶ Open your **PowerPoint** presentation called **Belgian Sheepdogs** and go to **Slide 2** – you are going to include speaker notes for this slide.

▶ Go to the **View** menu and select **Notes Page**.

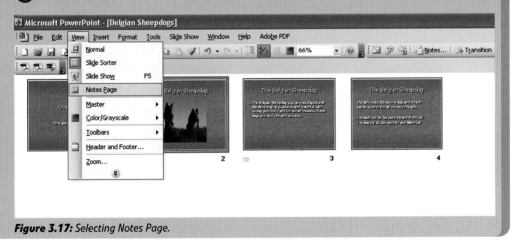

Figure 3.17: *Selecting Notes Page.*

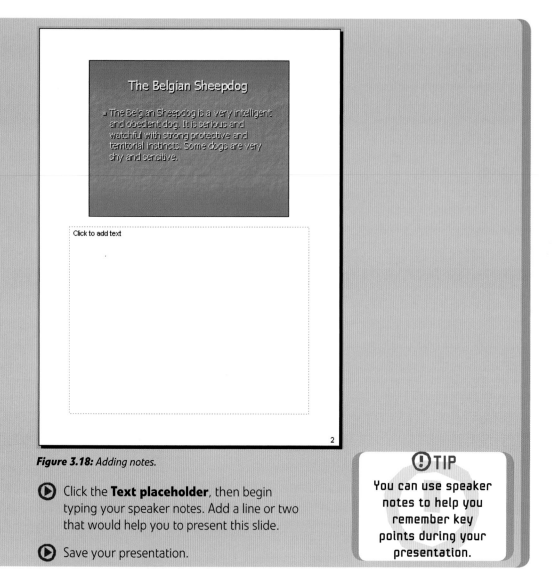

Figure 3.18: *Adding notes.*

▶ Click the **Text placeholder**, then begin typing your speaker notes. Add a line or two that would help you to present this slide.

▶ Save your presentation.

Error checks

Before you show your presentation to an audience, you should check it for any inconsistencies of style and for any grammar and/or spelling errors; this is sometimes called proof reading.

There is a **spelling check** function within the presentation software. However, errors in embedded objects such as charts and in word art, or inserted documents, will not be checked.

Key terms

Spelling check

A feature within the program to highlight and correct errors in spelling and grammar.

Activity 7: Checking for errors...

In this activity you will:

● check your presentation for spelling errors.

 On the **Standard** toolbar, click **Spelling**.

 Select the option you want for each word the spelling check stops on. You can change it to the suggested spelling, ignore it, add it to the custom dictionary or add it to the AutoCorrect list.

The Spelling icon.

Style check

When style checking is on in a presentation, you can check your presentation for consistency in punctuation, capitalisation and visual elements such as the minimum point size for text.

Style checks can check for the following:

● consistent capitalisation, such as the use of title caps or sentence caps, for title text and body text
● consistent use of end punctuation for titles and body text
● maximum number of font styles
● minimum font size for title text and body text
● maximum number of bulleted items in a list
● maximum number of text lines in title text or per list item.

Printing handouts

It can be a good idea to print out a selection of slides that you can give to your audience after you have completed your presentation.

Activity 8: Printing handouts...

In this activity you will:

● print out a selection of slides as handouts.

 Click **File** on the menu bar and then select **Print**. The **Print dialogue** box should appear.

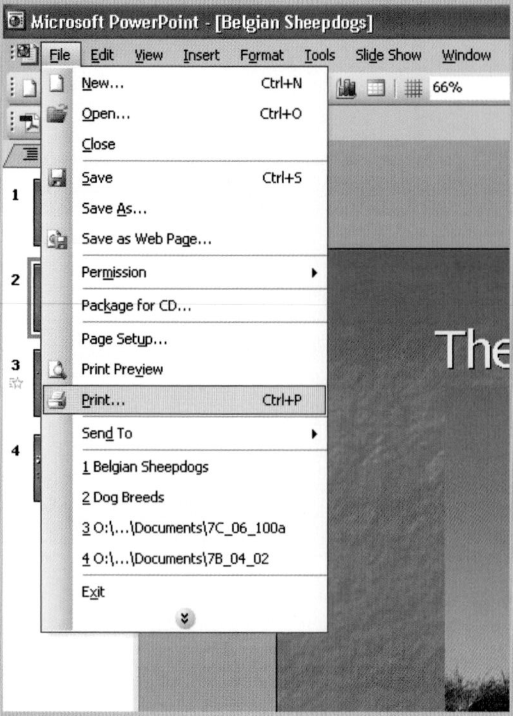

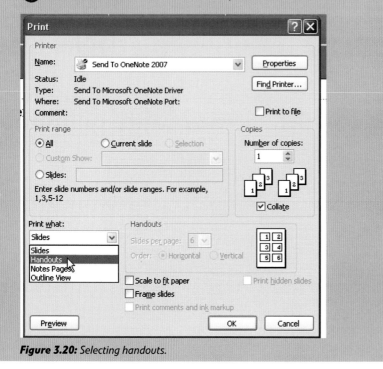

Figure 3.19: *Selecting print options.*

▶ Select the radio button **All** in the print range section to print all the slides.

▶ Click the drop-down box in the **Print what** section.

▶ Select **Handouts** from the list of options.

Figure 3.20: *Selecting handouts.*

▶ Click the drop-down box in the **Handouts** section.

▶ Select **4 slides per page** from the list of options.

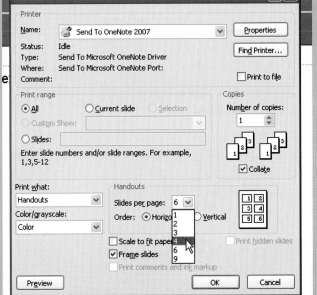

Figure 3.21: *Selecting the number of Slides per page.*

▶ Click **OK** to save your selections and print your handouts.

▶ Print your handouts.

Portfolio evidence

Based on the topic area that you have chosen in conjunction with your teacher or tutor, use the 'How to achieve' section at the beginning of this chapter to guide you in completing your presentation and including the necessary elements at the level towards which you are working.

The previous sections have given you some indication of how you could go about creating a business presentation, and the types of things that you need to think about when you are putting it together. You should think about:

● the appropriate elements for your presentation according to the information you need to share
● a consistent style
● the use of appropriate effects
● adding concise speaker notes which could be used for handouts
● the process of checking your document for errors.

CHAPTER 4

→ Assessment Objective 4

Producing Business Documents

Overview:

In this chapter, you will select and use tools and facilities in word processing or desktop publishing (DTP) software to produce a variety of business documents.

You will learn about a range of business documents that a business might use. You will learn how to add graphics, logos and different font styles to enhance your documents. You will learn about document templates and how to edit them for your own use. You will also learn how to use mail merge facilities to help you work more effectively.

> In order to complete the activities in this chapter you will need access to a number of additional files. These files are contained in the Chapter 4 Resources zip file which can be downloaded from the OCR Nationals in ICT (Units 1 and 21) Student Resources page on the Payne-Gallway website: www.payne-gallway.co.uk.

- **dog pic.jpg**
- **Company Letter.doc**
- **Address Book.mdb**
- **Dog Products.xls**

How this assessment objective will be assessed...

- You will need to produce a minimum of three business documents.
- You need to provide evidence of your various documents produced in word processing or DTP software only, for example:
  - printout(s) of your documents
  - screenshot(s) of each different technique used to create and check the documents
  - screenshot(s) to show the techniques used to obtain elements from external devices like a scanner or digital camera.

Skills to use...

You will need to:

- create a range of business documents
- enter text, tables and images using the keyboard, mouse or other input device

- import tables and graphic images, graphs and charts
- use formatting tools
- use delete, cut, copy and paste functions
- use spelling and grammar checkers
- use mail merge functions
- use headers and footers.

How to achieve...

Pass requirements

P1 You should create at least three business documents with one being a letter.

P2 You should check the documents using a spelling checker.

P3 You should use some formatting features such as font style and size and paragraph justification.

P4 You should include graphics from more than one source in at least one of your documents

Merit requirements

M1 You should create at least four types of business document, including a letter and a document of more than one page that includes tables, graphs and charts created in another software application.

M2 You should include text, tables and graphics from a range of sources and position and format them accordingly.

M3 You should use spelling and grammar checks and edit the documents to improve and correct them.

M4 You should use a range of software tools and facilities alongside standard templates and create documents with a consistent layout

Distinction requirements

D1 You should create at least four types of business document, including a mailmerged letter and a document of several pages including tables, graphs and charts created in other software.

D2 You should include graphics from a wide range of sources.

D3 You should design a consistent house style and use an extensive range of software tools and facilities.

D4 You should insert fields, including date and document information.

D5 You should use spelling and grammar checkers and proof read your documents so that they are of a near professional standard.

D6 You should insert fields in your documents including date and document information.

Types of business documents

Clear, effective business documents are important for the reputation and success of a company and its employees.

In a survey of 1000 company managers, 80 per cent said they decided not to interview job candidates because of poor grammar, spelling or punctuation in curriculum vitaes (CVs) or covering letters. Ninety-nine percent of these managers said that poor writing and grammar badly affected an employee's chances for promotion.

There are many examples of the types of business documents produced by desktop publishing (DTP) and word processing (WP) software. Examples listed below include:

- business letters
- memos
- reports
- agendas/minutes
- flyers
- business cards
- newsletters/factsheets
- invoices.

Business letters

A letter is often the first type of communication you will receive from a company. It is considered to be a formal document which bears the company address and logo and until a relationship is formed between the sender and recipient, a letter is perhaps seen as more appropriate than an email.

Because it is often the first communication, the recipient bases their opinion about the company on it: if the letter does not conform to your expectations of a professional looking business document, you may consider not doing business with that company. So getting the format right is very important.

When writing business letters, you must pay special attention to the layout, font and language used.

The most traditional and common layout for the body of a business letter is known as block format where the entire letter is left justified and single spaced except for a double space between paragraphs. However, as with everything, there are trends and fashions that affect styles and you may well have seen many letters that use fully justified paragraphs and no punctuation. Either way is a fully acceptable way to present your business document.

As well as the body of the letter, you also need to consider all of the following elements – there are some strict rules to follow:

- **Date**
  The date line is used to indicate the date the letter was written. However, if your letter is completed over a number of days, use the date on which it was finished in the date line. Including a date is important as it is often used to identify the exact letter you are replying to. For instance, replies to letters often start with 'In reference to your letter of [date]…'.

- **Sender's address**
  Including the address of the sender is optional. However, if you choose to include the sender's address, place the address one line above the date, in the top right-hand corner of the page. You should not include the sender's name or title, as it is included in the letter's closing.

Inside address

The inside address is the recipient's address and, unlike with the sender's address, you should include the name of the person you are sending the letter to above the address. This address should be written one line below the date on the left-hand side of the page, just above the salutation line.

Salutation line

The salutation line is the greeting line and is used to address the recipient of the letter. Use the same name as the inside address, including the personal title, Mr or Dr, for example. If you know the person and typically address them by their first name, it is acceptable to use only the first name in the salutation (i.e. Dear Lucy). In all other cases, however, use the personal title and full name. Leave one line blank after the salutation.

Body

Use single spacing and left or fully justify each paragraph within the body of the letter. Leave a blank line between each paragraph.

When writing a business letter, remember that being clear and concise is very important. Each paragraph of your letter should have a purpose and here is a suggestion of what you might include in different paragraphs. In the first paragraph, consider a friendly opening and then a statement around the main point of why you are sending the letter, for example, I am writing to complain; to congratulate you; to inform you. The next paragraph should begin expanding on the main point providing the details of why you are, for example, complaining; congratulating or informing. In the next few paragraphs, provide any background information and supporting details. The closing paragraph should restate the purpose of the letter and, in some cases, request some type of action.

Closing

The closing should be **left justified** and appear at the same horizontal point as the date and one line after the last paragraph. Capitalise the first word only, i.e. Thank you, Yours faithfully or Yours sincerely (these are the most common ways to close a business letter) and leave four lines between the closing and the sender's name for a signature. If a comma follows the salutation, a comma should follow the closing; otherwise, there is no punctuation after the closing.

Key terms

Left justified

Arranging text and/or images to the left-hand margin. (If text is **right justified**, the text and/or images will be arranged to the right-hand margin.)

> **⊙TIP**
> Use Yours faithfully after a salutation line of Dear Sir/Madam and Yours sincerely after a salutation line of, for example, Dear Mrs Smith.

Enclosures

If you have enclosed any documents along with the letter, such as a CV, you indicate this simply by typing Enc, which stands for 'enclosures' one line below the closing. As an option, you may list the name of each document you are including in the envelope. For instance, if you have included many documents and need to ensure that the recipient is aware of each document, it may be a good idea to list the names.

Memos

Memos are often used within companies to give short informal notifications of, for example, meetings or company changes.

Memos are most effective when they connect the purpose of the writer with the interests and needs of the reader.

Standard memos are divided into segments to organise the information into a simple and easy to read format and to help achieve the writer's purpose of providing concise information. The parts of a memo include:

- **The heading segment**
The heading segment follows this general format:

      TO: (readers' names and job titles)
      FROM: (your name and job title)
      DATE: (complete and current date)
      SUBJECT: (what the memo is about)

- **The main segment**
The purpose of a memo is usually found in the opening paragraphs and is presented in three parts: the context and problem, the specific assignment or task and the purpose of the memo in terms of how to solve the problem.

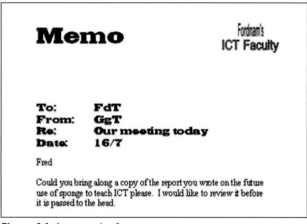

Figure 4.1: *An example of a memo.*

Reports

Reports are formal documents used in business to feed back information to a group of people, for example, the financial performance of the business to shareholders. Other uses include documenting market research, presenting new product ideas and reporting workflows, for example, maintenance carried out by teams. Reports have to be factual and will usually contain data to justify the conclusions made; this is often in the form of images and graphics such as tables and graphs.

Often a report is the only contact that people will have with the work that you are reporting on so the quality of the writing and how well you convey your findings is very important and there is a format for writing reports.

Reports are generally divided up into sections. Each section has a specific purpose and often there are specific guidelines for formatting each section. Companies usually produce a style manual to show the structure of all reports produced by the business.

Generally, a report will include the following sections:

- title page
- summary
- table of contents
- introduction
- body
- recommendations
- references
- appendices.

Agendas/Minutes

An agenda sets out the topics that will be discussed at a meeting and is often emailed to those attending the meeting before the meeting date to give everyone time to think about the topics being discussed or read any attached documents. A section called AOB (Any Other Business) is generally the last topic on an agenda – it gives people the chance to add any other points they want to raise. The agenda should be strictly followed within the time set out for the meeting which is also shown on the agenda, along with the place of the meeting and the names of those who will be attending.

The minutes of a meeting is a written document that records what was discussed at the meeting and by whom. It also records any action to be taken as a result of the meeting and a date by which it should be carried out.

Flyers

A flyer is a document designed to advertise an event or product. It might be used at an exhibition or mailed to a list of potentially interested customers. It will include very little information focussing on the basic facts and often includes graphics to attract attention to it.

Figure 4.2: *An example of a flyer.*

Business cards

Business cards normally include the business name and logo, the employee's name and title and full contact information. The contact information can be phone numbers, email addresses, websites and fax numbers. This is everything a potential or current client needs to know in order to get in touch with the employee. It is important that the logo appears on the card exactly as it does on letter headings and any other company stationery: this is the way that the company advertises itself and continuity is very important to help clients to instantly recognise it from other competition.

Business cards are very convenient to use. They are small, lightweight and can fit in a pocket, purse or wallet. This makes them an excellent tool for business. They act as a reminder and hopefully as a prompt to contact you when you trying to attract work for your business.

Figure 4.3: *An example of a business card.*

Newsletters/Factsheets

This is an informal way of communicating events and information happening around the company to its employees. It is often sent as an electronic document.

Invoices

This is a request for payment which details the goods purchased, the amount of each and the total charge. It is written on paper that includes the company logo and address details to reinforce the fact that it is a genuine document.

Large companies use design studios to professionally design their logos and document headings but smaller companies might use a DTP software program to do this.

Logos and house style

As you can see, a company can produce a whole range of documents, each with a very different purpose. However, one thing will remain the same on each of them and that is their logo. Each company has its own logo so that it can be instantly recognised and picked out from other companies. The business documents created within that company also carry the company logo which may be a combination of an image and slogan or company name.

Another way in which companies maintain their corporate identity when producing and communicating through many different types of documents is to use a house style. A house style is a set of defined formatting which is applied to all documents. It covers elements such as:

- use of colour
- font style
- font size
- font colour
- layout of documents
- headings
- email signatures and sign offs

The use of a house style is a relatively simple yet effective way to ensure that your documents are consistent and professional.

Creating and formatting business documents

Publication software is used to communicate effectively using a standard method; it makes it easier to produce page layouts for documents and web pages.

There are two types of publication software which are commonly used. These are word processing and DTP applications. There are many similarities but also some differences between the two types of software. You will need to choose the right type of application for your needs.

If you are producing a document which is mainly text but could require the inclusion of a few graphics then you would probably use a word processing program.

There are many document templates that you can choose from to help you lay out your document. A document template is a pre-formatted document in which you can add text or graphics. Normally you select a template before entering text. If you do not select a template, the software selects one for you, usually a plain template. Templates contain formatting information such as margins, line spacing, font type and size.

If you are unsure of how to use the template you can use a document wizard to provide step-by-step guidance to help you when entering and formatting the text and graphics.

> **⊙TIP**
>
> **Microsoft Word provides a range of ready-made templates. These can be accessed by selecting File, New and then selecting the template of your choice. More templates can be downloaded from the Microsoft website.**

Desktop publishing (DTP) was originally developed to enable publishers to produce high quality posters, newsletters, magazines and leaflets. Many companies use DTP software to produce their own in-house publicity material. DTP has many functions that make changing the layout of text and graphics quick and easy. It is a good choice for documents that include lots of graphics.

Using DTP and word processing software means that:

- documents can be saved on the computer, rather than as paper versions, which take up office space
- saved documents can be stored for review and editing to create new versions of the documents for other projects
- templates can be created for efficiency.

For a business this means that work can be carried out more efficiently and at a lower cost.

In Activities 1 and 2 below you are going to produce a fact sheet about a breed of dog using a word processing package – we have chosen a word processing package because the document includes more text than graphics. You will be inserting some text, a table and an image into your document.

Activity 1: Entering text and tables into a business document...

In this activity you will:

- enter text
- create a table.

 Load the word processor and create a new blank document.

 Make sure the cursor is positioned at the top of the document.

 Enter the heading: **Belgian Sheepdogs**.

 Start a new paragraph by pressing the **Enter** key several times to create a space between the heading and the main text.

 Enter the text shown below:

The Belgian Sheepdog is a very intelligent and obedient dog. It is serious and watchful with strong protective and territorial instincts. Some dogs are very shy or sensitive.

 Press the **Enter** key twice to create a blank line.

 Check your work carefully then enter the second paragraph below:

Belgian Sheepdogs may often display herding behaviour, such as chasing and circling. This is a very demanding dog and it needs an experienced owner, as it can be difficult to control unless the owner knows how to handle it.

 Click **File** on the menu bar, then click **Save**.

Figure 4.4: Saving your file.

 The **Save As** dialogue box appears.

 Save your file as **Belgian Sheepdogs**.

Figure 4.5: The Save As dialogue box.

To create a table:

▶ Place the cursor at the end of the second paragraph.

▶ Press the **Enter** key twice to create a blank space at the end of the paragraph.

▶ Select **Table** on the menu bar, then select **Insert, Table**. The **Insert Table** dialogue box appears.

▶ In the **Number of columns** box type **2**.

▶ In the **Number of rows** box enter **5**, then click **OK**.

Insert Table	☒
Table size	
Number of columns:	2
Number of rows:	5
AutoFit behavior	
⦿ Fixed column width:	Auto
◯ AutoFit to contents	
◯ AutoFit to window	
Table style: Table Grid	AutoFormat...
☐ Remember dimensions for new tables	
OK	Cancel

Figure 4.6: *The Insert Table dialogue box.*

▶ You should now see a table appear in your document. Copy the text in the table below into your document:

Breed name	Belgian Shepherd (Malinois)
Category	Pastoral
Average lifespan	9–15 years
Average food cost	£4–£7.50 per week
Average puppy price	£300–£500

> **!TIP**
> You can use tables to align numbers in columns and then sort them into different orders.

Save your file.

When giving information about a subject it is often easier for people to understand if you use a graphic as well.

Here are some ways of obtaining images:

- **Scanned images** An image scanner electronically **captures** text and images and converts them into **digital data** that can be processed by a computer. A scanner is used where a picture already exists in hard copy, for example, a photograph. You should be able to scan a photo to use in your work.
- **Digital images** Digital cameras record photographs in the form of digital data. The digital pictures are stored directly in the camera's memory and can be transferred to a computer. The advantage of digital images is that they are already in a format that can be inserted in your work. However, sometimes the images are too large and need to be reduced. You should be able to insert a digital image into your own work.

- **Drawing programs** Drawing programs allow you to produce graphic images for use in your work. Some programs have **drawing tools** within them.
- **Graphing programs** There are a number of programs that will automatically produce graphs and charts that can then be inserted into documents.
- **Clipart** Collections of pre-drawn images are available in clipart libraries. You can access these from most of the programs that you will be using. You should be able to use clipart images in your work.
- **Adding an image** Activity 2 below shows how you can insert an image into a document from a saved file. There may also be instances when copying and pasting is useful, for instance, if you need to insert a graph into a word processed document.

To achieve this unit you must use graphics from a range of sources, these could include clipart, scanned images or images from the Web. You should add at least 2 of these to your documents.

Key terms

Captures

Copying an image from a computer screen.

Digital data

Real information that is converted into binary numeric form.

Drawing tools

Features within software that helps to create drawings and other images.

Activity 2: Adding a graphic image to a business document...

In this activity you will:

- add a graphic image to your factsheet
- insert a table from a spreadsheet
- insert a chart.

▶ Open the factsheet **Belgian Sheepdogs** that you created in Activity 1. Press the **Enter** key twice to create a space after the table.

▶ Click **Insert** on the menu bar.

▶ Click **Picture, From File...** The **Insert dialogue** box will appear. The image file you need is called **dog pic.jpg**. You should have downloaded this graphic file at the beginning of this unit.

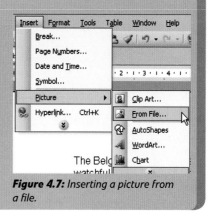

Figure 4.7: Inserting a picture from a file.

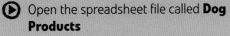 Click on this file and then click **Insert**. The image will be inserted in your document. Your document should look like the one shown in Figure 4.8.

The Belgian Sheepdog is a very intelligent and obedient dog. It is serious and watchful with strong protective and territorial instincts. Some dogs are very shy or sensitive.

Belgian Sheepdogs may often display herding behaviour, such as chasing and circling. This is a very demanding dog and it needs an experienced owner, as it can be difficult to control unless the owner knows how to handle him.

Breed name	Belgian Shepherd (Malinois)
Category	Pastoral
Average life span	9 – 15 years
Average food cost	£4 - £7.50 per week
Average puppy price	£300 - £500

Figure 4.8: *The finished document.*

To insert a table created in a spreadsheet:

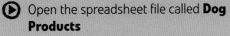 Open the spreadsheet file called **Dog Products**

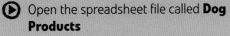 Select the data in columns A1 to and B7.

> **⊙TIP**
> You can also use tables to create interesting page layouts.

	Microsoft Excel - Dog Products

File Edit View Insert Format Tools Data Window

A1   *fx* Description

	A	B
1	**Description**	**Price**
2	Muzzle	£5.50
3	Dog Agility Hurdle	£19.99
4	Dog Agility Starter Kit	£49.99
5	Dog Whistle	£2.70
6	Dog Bed	£27.99
7	Activity Ball	£6.99

Figure 4.9: Copy data.

▶ Click **Copy**

▶ Click in the document called **Belgian Sheepdogs,** at the end of the document.

▶ Press **Enter** to insert a line.

▶ Type the title **Products for Dogs** in the document.

▶ Press **Enter** to insert a line.

▶ Click **Paste** to insert the new table

▶ Save your file.

To insert a chart:

▶ Open the spreadsheet file called **Dog Products**

▶ Select the chart by clicking in the **Chart Area**

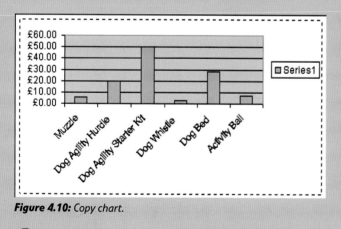

Figure 4.10: Copy chart.

▶ Click **Copy**

▶ Click in the document called **Belgian Sheepdogs,** at the end of the document.

⏵ Press **Enter** to insert a line.

⏵ Click **Paste Special** and select **Picture** to insert the chart into your document.

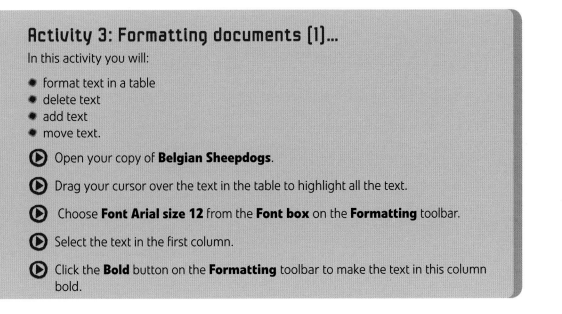

Figure 4.11: *Paste special.*

⏵ Save your file.

Formatting tools

Most word processing and DTP software allows you to change the appearance of text or images in a document. Some of the formatting tools available are shown in the toolbar below:

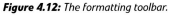

Figure 4.12: *The formatting toolbar.*

Activity 3: Formatting documents [1]...

In this activity you will:

● format text in a table
● delete text
● add text
● move text.

⏵ Open your copy of **Belgian Sheepdogs**.

⏵ Drag your cursor over the text in the table to highlight all the text.

⏵ Choose **Font Arial size 12** from the **Font box** on the **Formatting** toolbar.

⏵ Select the text in the first column.

⏵ Click the **Bold** button on the **Formatting** toolbar to make the text in this column bold.

Your table should now look like the one shown below:

Breed name	Belgian Shepherd (Malinois)
Category	Pastoral
Average life span	9 – 15 years
Average food cost	£4 - £7.50 per week
Average puppy price	£300 - £500

***Figure 4.13:** The finished table.*

To delete text:

 In the first paragraph highlight the text **Some dogs are very shy or sensitive**.

 Press the **Backspace** or the **Delete** key on the keyboard. The highlighted text will disappear.

To add text:

 Position your cursor between the first and the second paragraph.

 Type in the following information:

The Belgian Sheepdog has a lot of energy and needs a job to do. Belgian Sheepdogs tend to bond strongly with one or two people.

To move text:

 Highlight the first sentence in the third paragraph.

 Right click on the highlighted text.

 Select **Cut** from the list of options.

 The text will disappear from the document.

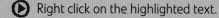

***Figure 4.14:** Cutting text.*

 Place your cursor at the end of the first paragraph, after the word **instincts**.

 Right click with your mouse and select **Paste** from the list of options.

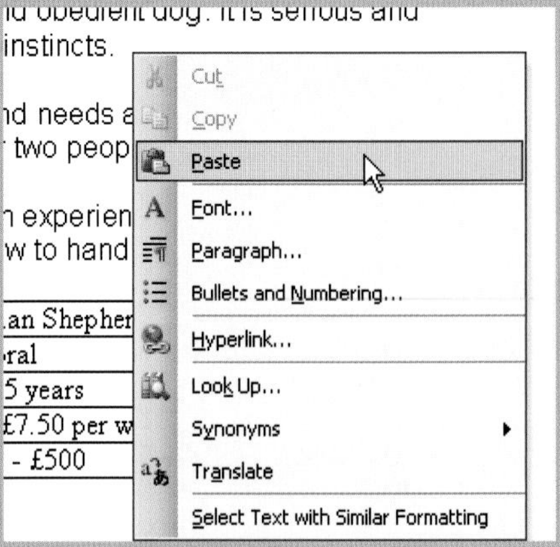

...d obedient dog. It is serious and
instincts.

...d needs a
...r two peop

...h experien
...w to hand

| Cut |
| Copy |
| Paste |
| Font... |
| Paragraph... |
| Bullets and Numbering... |
| Hyperlink... |
| Look Up... |
| Synonyms ▶ |
| Translate |
| Select Text with Similar Formatting |

...an Shepher
...ral
...5 years
...£7.50 per w
... - £500

Figure 4.15: *Pasting text.*

⊘ **TIP**

You can use keyboard shortcuts instead to copy and paste text and graphics in a document.

Your document should now look like the one shown below:

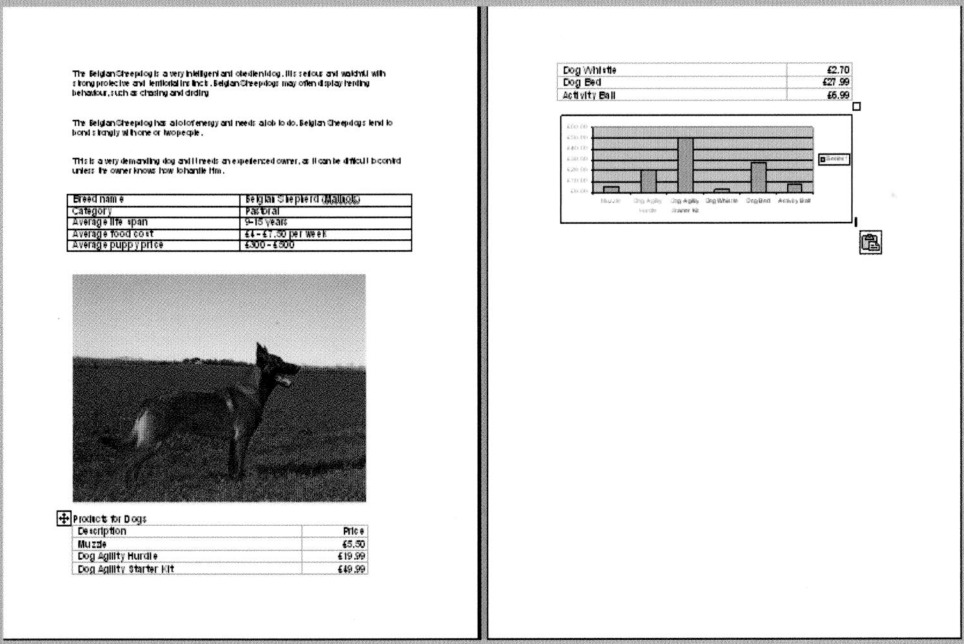

Figure 4.16: *The finished document.*

▶ Save your document.

⊘ **TIP**

To format an image you can right click on it and use the Format Picture menu to change the appearance of the image.

Activity 4: Formatting documents (2)...

In this activity you will:

- add a bulleted list to a document
- indent a list
- carry out a 'find and replace'
- add a page break.

To add bullets:

▶ Press the **Enter** key three times to add a space under the photograph.

▶ Type the list below into your document.

The nose should be black.

The eyes should be dark brown, of medium size and almond-shaped.

Their ears should be of small to medium size, triangular and set high.

The neck should be well-muscled and slightly arched.

The back legs should be powerful and well-muscled.

The front feet should be round and tight with well-arched toes and the back feet slightly oval in shape.

Their movement should be light and brisk.

The tail should be of medium length.

▶ Highlight the list in your document.

▶ Click the **Bullets** button on the **Formatting** toolbar.

The Bullets icon.

> **⊗TIP**
>
> You can use a graphical image or picture instead of the bullets. You can also use a numbered list.

To indent a list:

▶ Click the **Increase Indent** button to indent the list.

The Increase Indent icon.

To find and replace:

You are going to find the word **sheepdog** and replace it with the word **shepherd**.

▶ Click **Edit** on the menu bar and then click **Replace**.

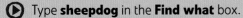

Figure 4.17: Click on Replace.

The **Find Replace** dialogue box will appear.

▶ Type **sheepdog** in the **Find what** box.

▶ Type **shepherd** in the **Replace with** box.

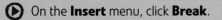

Figure 4.18: The Find and Replace dialogue box.

▶ Click **Replace All**. Four replacements will be made.

▶ Click **OK**.

To add a page break:

▶ Place your cursor at the beginning of the list, next to the word **The**. This is where the page break will be placed.

▶ On the **Insert** menu, click **Break**.

▶ Click **Page break**.

Figure 4.19: Adding a page break.

Your document should now look like the one in Figure 4.20 below:

 Save your document.

The Belgian Shepherd is a very intelligent and obedient dog. It is serious and watchful with strong protective and territorial instincts. Belgian Shepherds may often display herding behaviour, such as chasing and circling.

The Belgian Shepherd has a lot of energy and needs a job to do. Belgian Shepherds tend to bond strongly with one or two people.

This is a very demanding dog and it needs an experienced owner, as it can be difficult to control unless the owner knows how to handle him.

Breed name	Belgian Shepherd (Malinois)
Category	Pastoral
Average life span	9 – 15 years
Average food cost	£4 - £7.50 per week
Average puppy price	£300 - £500

- The nose should be black.
- The eyes should be dark brown, of medium size and almond-shaped
- Their ears should be of small to medium size, triangular and set high
- The neck should be well muscled and slightly arched
- The back legs should be powerful and well muscled
- The front feet should be round and tight with well-arched toes and the back feet slightly oval in shape
- Their movement should be light and brisk
- The tail should be of medium length

Figure 4.20: *The finished document.*

> **⊘TIP**
>
> You can insert a section break, instead of a page break, to divide the document into sections so that you can vary the layout of a document between pages.

Quality and professionalism

To give any company a professional image, all documents produced should be checked for grammar and spelling errors before they are sent out to customers. However, you should note that checking the spelling of words cannot correct errors in punctuation or usage, nor will it find words which are misused but spelled correctly. For example, a paragraph could have many floors (flaws) but this would be passed by the spell checker. Therefore, proof reading your document carefully is still very important.

Activity 5: Carrying out a spelling and grammar check...

In this activity you will:

- use the built in spelling and grammar checker to find and correct errors.

 Open a new word processing document.

 Type the following text into your document:

> The Belgian Shepdog responds best to firm, but not harsh training from an experienced owners. If you are harsh or overbearing they may become uncooperative.

▶ Any possible spelling errors will be highlighted by a red line, grammar errors are shown by a green line.

▶ Click the **Spelling and Grammar** button on the toolbar.

▶ The **Spelling and Grammar** dialogue box will appear:

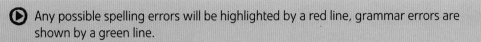

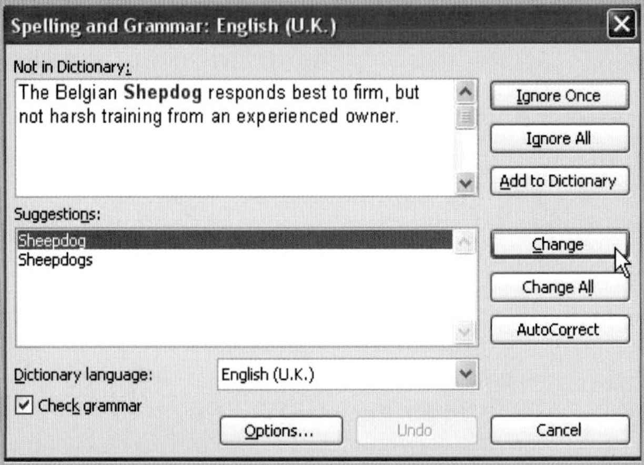

The Spelling and Grammar check icon.

Figure 4.21: *The Spelling and Grammar dialogue box.*

▶ Click the **Change** button to accept and make the corrections.

▶ Select the second option given.

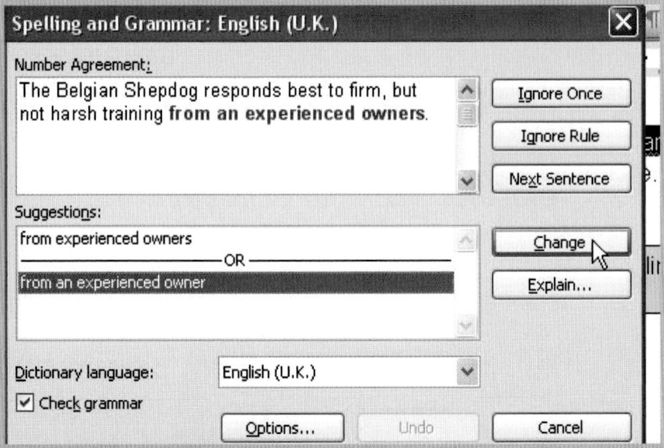

Figure 4.22: *Selecting the second option.*

▶ Click the **Change** button to accept the correction.

▶ Save your work.

⊕ TIP

You can customise the spell checker. For example, you can have the spell checker ignore words in uppercase, words that contain numbers and Internet addresses, etc.

Once a document is created on the company headed paper, and has been checked for accuracy, it may need to be mailed to several people at the same time. To do this, word processing packages have a function called mail merge.

Mail merging

Mail merge is a quick way of producing separate letters for a range of different people. The letter will contain the same text but each individual letter can be personalised with individual names and addresses. This means that the letter only has to be written once but can be addressed to thousands of different people.

For example, the company NW may wish to:

- remind their members that their subscription renewal is due for payment
- invite a group of people to the same event, for example, a sheepdog show
- advertise a new service for payment to a large number of their existing members.

Mail merge creates more personalised documents by combining information from a mailing list or database with a standard letter (the main document). The text within the standard letter does not change, except where special **merge fields** or markers for the name, address or other information to be added have been inserted.

The list of names and addresses is called the data source.

The following activity shows you how to carry out a mail merge.

Key terms

Merge fields

Identifies the data to be inserted from a selected source into a specific place in a document.

Activity 6: Creating a mail merged letter...

In this activity you will:

- create a mail merged letter.

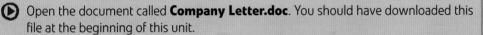 Open the document called **Company Letter.doc**. You should have downloaded this file at the beginning of this unit.

 Select **Letters and Mailings** from the **Tools** menu.

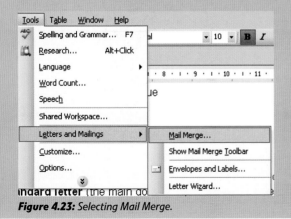

Figure 4.23: Selecting Mail Merge.

▶ The **Mail Merge** task pane will appear.

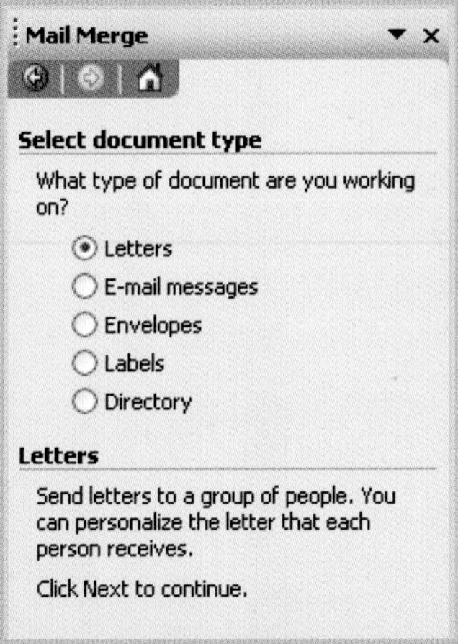

Figure 4.24: *The Mail Merge task pane.*

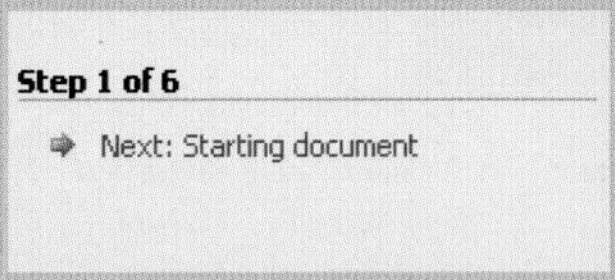

Figure 4.25: *Starting a Mail Merge.*

▶ Click **Next** at the bottom of the pane to continue.

▶ Click **Next: Select Recipients**.

▶ Click **Browse** and find the Access database file called **Address Book.mdb**. You should have downloaded this file at the beginning of this unit.

▶ Click **Select All** and then select **OK**.

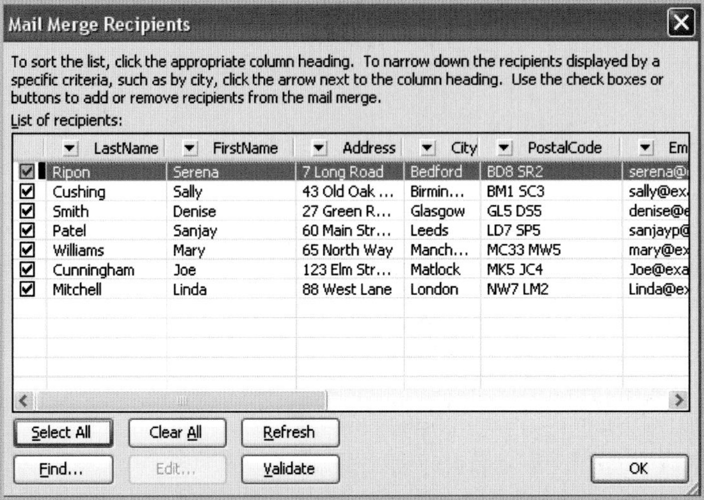

	LastName	FirstName	Address	City	PostalCode	Em
☑	Ripon	Serena	7 Long Road	Bedford	BD8 SR2	serena@
☑	Cushing	Sally	43 Old Oak ...	Birmin...	BM1 SC3	sally@ex
☑	Smith	Denise	27 Green R...	Glasgow	GL5 DS5	denise@e
☑	Patel	Sanjay	60 Main Str...	Leeds	LD7 SP5	sanjayp@
☑	Williams	Mary	65 North Way	Manch...	MC33 MW5	mary@ex
☑	Cunningham	Joe	123 Elm Str...	Matlock	MK5 JC4	Joe@exa
☑	Mitchell	Linda	88 West Lane	London	NW7 LM2	Linda@ex

Figure 4.26: *Mail Merge Recipients list.*

▶ In the task pane click **Next: Write your letter**.

▶ Highlight the text **Type your letter** here and press **Backspace**.

NW Ltd
123 North Street
Anytown
NK4 5AT
Tel: 01234 56789
e-mail: nkw@example.co.uk

February 23, 2007

«AddressBlock»

«GreetingLine»

Type your letter here.

Sincerely,

[Click **here** and type your name]
[Click **here** and type job title]

Figure 4.27: Highlighting the text.

▶ Type the text below into your letter:

Thank you for renewing your policy for a further 12 months. Please find enclosed your new policy document.

Please do call us if you have any further enquiries.

▶ Highlight the fields **Click here and type your name** and **Click here and type job title**.

▶ Type a name and job title for the sender.

[Click **here** and type your name]
[Click **here** and type job title]

Figure 4.28: Highlight these fields.

▶ Click **Next: Preview your letter**.

▶ Click **Next: Complete the merge**.

▶ Save and close your letter.

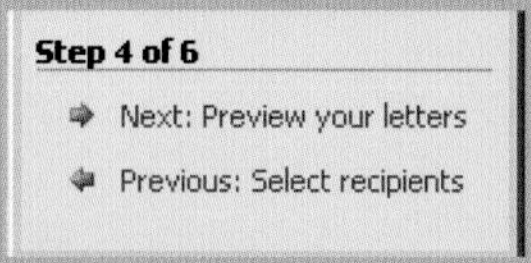

Step 4 of 6
➡ Next: Preview your letters
⬅ Previous: Select recipients

Figure 4.29: Click 'Next: Preview your letter'.

▶ Your finished letter should look like the one shown below:

NW Ltd
123 North Street
Anytown
NK4 5AT
Tel: 01234 56789
e-mail: nkw@example.co.uk

23 May 2007

Serena Ripon
7 Long Road
Bedford BD8 SR2

Dear Serena

Thank you for renewing your policy for a further 12 months. Please find enclosed your new policy document.

Please do call us if you have any further enquiries.

Sincerely

N Williams
Company Manager

Figure 4.30: *The final mail merged letter.*

(⏻ **TIP**)
If you are not using headed paper on which to print your letter, you could make use of the header feature that appears in word processing software.

Headers and footers

Headers and footers are useful for business documents whenever you need to repeat the same text or graphics on each page of your document

A header or footer may contain the document title, page numbers, the name of the document author, a logo, the date or time, etc.

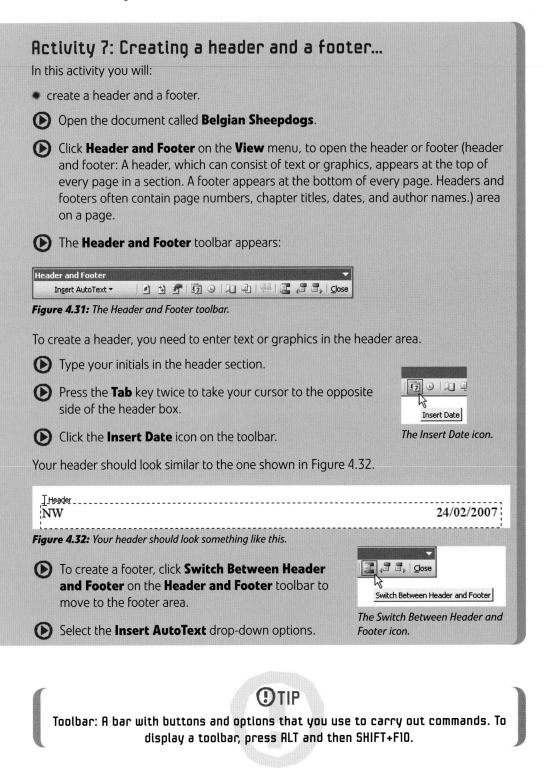

Activity 7: Creating a header and a footer...

In this activity you will:

● create a header and a footer.

▶ Open the document called **Belgian Sheepdogs**.

▶ Click **Header and Footer** on the **View** menu, to open the header or footer (header and footer: A header, which can consist of text or graphics, appears at the top of every page in a section. A footer appears at the bottom of every page. Headers and footers often contain page numbers, chapter titles, dates, and author names.) area on a page.

▶ The **Header and Footer** toolbar appears:

Figure 4.31: The Header and Footer toolbar.

To create a header, you need to enter text or graphics in the header area.

▶ Type your initials in the header section.

▶ Press the **Tab** key twice to take your cursor to the opposite side of the header box.

▶ Click the **Insert Date** icon on the toolbar.

The Insert Date icon.

Your header should look similar to the one shown in Figure 4.32.

Header	
NW	24/02/2007

Figure 4.32: Your header should look something like this.

▶ To create a footer, click **Switch Between Header and Footer** on the **Header and Footer** toolbar to move to the footer area.

The Switch Between Header and Footer icon.

▶ Select the **Insert AutoText** drop-down options.

> ⓘTIP
>
> **Toolbar:** A bar with buttons and options that you use to carry out commands. To display a toolbar, press ALT and then SHIFT+F10.

▶ Choose **Filename** from the list of options.

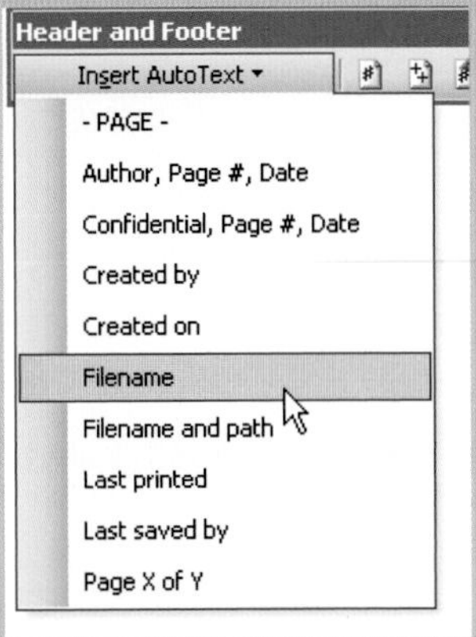

Figure 4.33: *Choose Filename from the Insert AutoText menu.*

▶ The name of your file will appear in the footer of your document.

Your footer should look something like the one shown in Figure 4.34.

Figure 4.34: *Your footer should look something like this.*

▶ When you finish, click **Close** on the **Header and Footer** toolbar and save your work.

⊘TIP

You can use the same header and footer throughout the document or you can change the header and footer for different sections of the document.

Portfolio evidence

Based on the topic area that you have chosen in conjunction with your teacher or tutor, use the 'How to achieve' section at the beginning of this chapter to guide you in creating a variety of business documents and including the necessary elements at the level towards which you are working.

The previous sections have given you some indication of how you could go about creating different types of business documents, and the types of things that you need to think about when creating them. You should think about:

- the correct type of document according to the information you need to share
- the correct format for the type of document you have chosen
- the house style or company identity
- whether or not the language used is appropriate for your audience
- the process of checking your document for errors.

CHAPTER ⑤

→ *Assessment Objective 5*

Business Spreadsheets

Overview:

In this chapter, you will learn how to produce and use simple business spreadsheets. You will use the spreadsheet facilities to create and edit effective and accurate spreadsheets. You will use formatting options to improve them.

You will also learn how to change data to obtain different results in spreadsheets. You will use the preview and other print options to produce meaningful printouts of your completed spreadsheet.

How this assessment objective will be assessed...

● You will need to provide evidence that you are able to produce a business spreadsheet and change data to obtain different results.

● For a **Pass**, you will produce a spreadsheet that meets a simple business purpose. You will need to use some calculations on it. Your sheet must be well laid out with row and column headings. You should provide a printed copy of your spreadsheet at each stage of its development. For a **Merit**, you will provide evidence (including formula printouts) that you can change the format of numbers, column width and text, and use several formulas and at least one function. You will also need to provide evidence that you can delete and insert rows. For a **Distinction**, you will need to provide evidence that you can use more than one function. You must print out your spreadsheet in two formats, one showing the spreadsheet, the other showing the formulas. You should also be able to show that you understand options such as print orientation and gridlines.

Skills to use...

You will need to:

● use spreadsheet facilities to create a business spreadsheet
● edit spreadsheets
● use formatting options
● change data to obtain different results
● enter and replicate formulas (and display them)
● use preview and other print options
● use headers and footers.

How to achieve...

> **Pass requirements**
>
> **P1** You should create a very simple business spreadsheet using a limited number of calculations.
>
> **P2** You should use some formatting tools.
>
> **P3** You should change data to obtain different results.
>
> **P4** You should print out the spreadsheets.

Merit requirements

M1 You should create an effective business spreadsheet displaying accurate figures.

M2 You should add a title and appropriate row/column headings.

M3 You should use several different formulas and one function.

M4 You should use formatting tools.

M5 You should edit the spreadsheet by inserting/deleting rows.

M6 You should include formula printouts.

M7 You should preview and print out your spreadsheet using appropriate page orientation and number of pages.

Distinction requirements

D1 You should preview and print out your spreadsheet using appropriate page orientation and number of pages.

D2 You should use formulas efficiently and include more than one function.

D3 You should use appropriate headers and footers.

D4 You should set other print layout features appropriately.

Business spreadsheets

A hand-held calculator can be useful for making simple calculations in a business context. However, while calculators remember the numbers you have entered, you cannot see them, cannot verify their accuracy and it's difficult to re-do the whole calculation if you make an input error.

Spreadsheets, on the other hand, enable you to view all the numbers on a screen, make it easy to change numbers and calculations and even allow you to print a well-formatted report that can include graphs.

When you work on a spreadsheet, you create what is called a **worksheet**. A worksheet has columns and rows; each column is lettered and each row is numbered. This allows you to provide a location for each entry in the spreadsheet, called a cell reference. A cell reference is simply the letter from the column and the number from the row.

Key terms

Worksheet

A worksheet is the document produced by a spreadsheet program consisting of rows and columns; several worksheets in a set are referred to as a workbook.

Individual cells can contain:

- numbers – these are usually used where you want to perform a calculation
- text – this is used for labels
- a **formula** – this is used to tell the computer how to use the contents of cells in calculations.

One of the biggest advantages of the spreadsheet is the way it handles numbers and formulas in a worksheet. Formulas can be hidden, with only the results of these formulas appearing in a cell. Whenever you add or change something in a cell, the spreadsheet recalculates all of the formulas and displays the new figures.

Another advantage of spreadsheets is that, as well as entering your own formulas, you can use predefined formulas (called **functions**). Functions not only carry out mathematical calculations but can also add aspects such as the date, financial calculations and statistical calculations. This is extremely useful to businesses because it means they can set up a spreadsheet that calculates, for example, the number of sales for each product they sell – they can simply change or add new sales figures over time and the spreadsheet will automatically calculate the revenue (money) or profit made. This saves a lot of time and reduces the room for error.

Key terms

Formula

This is an equation that analyses data in a worksheet. Formulas perform operations such as addition and multiplication.

Function

A function is a predefined or 'built-in' formula. It can be used to perform simple or complex calculations, for example, the SUM function, which is used to add together ranges of cells.

Creating a basic spreadsheet

Your introduction to spreadsheets begins in the activity below where you are going to create your own spreadsheet. One of the most common spreadsheet applications used is Microsoft Excel but you can use the principles outlined in the activities in any spreadsheet package.

Activity 1: Creating a new spreadsheet...

In this activity you will:

- create a new spreadsheet
- enter data
- change the column width.

▶ Load your spreadsheet software.

▶ Open a new workbook.

▶ Highlight cell **A1** by clicking in it.

▶ Type in the heading **Sales Figures for July**. Column **A** will not be wide enough but you will learn how to change that in the next step.

▶ Highlight cell **A3** by clicking it.

▶ Type in the heading **Book Title**.

▶ Highlight cell **B3** and type in **North West**.

▶ Now work your way across row 3 entering the headings shown in Figure 5.1.

Don't worry if your headings run into each other and look a bit odd. You will be learning how to adjust the column widths later.

	A	B	C	D	E	F	G	H	I	J	K
1	Sales Figures for July										
2											
3	Book Title	North West	North East	South	Midlands	London	Wales	Nothern Ireland	Total Sales	Price	Income
4											
5											
6											
7											

Figure 5.1: Your new spreadsheet with column headings.

You are now going to enter data underneath the headings in each column, starting with column **A**.

▶ Click cell **A4**.

▶ Type **War of the Roses**.

▶ Press **Enter**. You will notice that the spreadsheet software automatically moves the cursor to the next cell down (**A5**).

> **!TIP**
>
> Make sure you either click in each individual cell, tab along to the cell you want or press Return before typing the text for each new cell.

▶ Work your way down column **A**, entering the rest of the book titles shown in Figure 5.2.

	A	B	C	D	E	F	G	H	I	J	K
1	Sales Figures for July										
2											
3	Book Title	North West	North East	South	Midlands	London	Wales	Nothern Ireland	Total Sales	Price	Income
4	War of the Roses										
5	The Deathly Hallows										
6	How to be the Best at Everything										
7	Grow your own Veg										
8	Restless										
9	Understanding the Weather										
10											

Figure 5.2: Your new spreadsheet with books added to column A.

You now need to change the width of column **A** so that all of the book titles can be seen.

▶ Put your mouse pointer on the line between the column headers **A** and **B**. You will notice that the pointer changes to a double headed arrow.

	A	B	C
1	Sales Figures for July		
2			
3	Book Title	North West	North East

Figure 5.3: The pointer changes to a double headed arrow.

> ► While the double headed arrows are shown, press and hold down the left mouse button and drag the mouse to the right. You will notice that the columns will start to widen. Do not let go of the mouse button until you can read all of the **Book Title** names in column A.

	A	B	C
1	Sales Figures for July		
2			
3	Book Title	North West	North East
4	War of the Roses		
5	The Deathly Hallows		
6	How to be the Best at Everything		
7	Grow your own Veg		
8	Restless		
9	Understanding the Weather		
10			

Figure 5.4: *Re-sized column A.*

> **! TIP**
>
> The ##### symbols appear if the column is too narrow to display the numeric contents of the cell.

You can also use another technique to change the width of columns.

> ► Position the mouse pointer on the line between the column headers **B** and **C**.

> ► When the mouse pointer changes to a double headed arrow, double click the left mouse button. You will notice that the column automatically adjusts itself to show the column headings.

> ► Widen all the rest of the columns in the same way.

> ► Save your spreadsheet with the filename **Book Sales Figures** by clicking on **File** and **Save As**.

	A	B	C	D	E	F	G	H	I	J	K
1	Sales Figures for July										
2											
3	Book Title	North West	North East	South	Midlands	London	Wales	Nothern Ireland	Total Sales	Price	Income
4	War of the Roses										
5	The Deathly Hallows										
6	How to be the Best at Everything										
7	Grow your own Veg										
8	Restless										
9	Understanding the Weather										
10											

Figure 5.5: *All the columns, auto adjusted.*

You now need to enter some numbers (sales figures) on your spreadsheet.

> ► Click on cell **B4**.

> ► Type in the number **570**.

> ► Press **Enter**.

> ► Work down column **B4**, entering all of the numbers shown in Figure 5.6.

	A	B	C	D
1	Sales Figures for July			
2				
3	Book Title	North West	North East	Sout
4	War of the Roses	570		
5	The Deathly Hallows	600		
6	How to be the Best at Everything	435		
7	Grow your own Veg	444		
8	Restless	500		
9	Understanding the Weather	234		
10				
11				

Figure 5.6: *Adding numbers to your worksheet.*

▶ Work your way down each column, entering all the numbers shown in Figure 5.7 below.

▶ Save your spreadsheet again.

	A	B	C	D	E	F	G	H	I	J	K
1	Sales Figures for July										
2											
3	Book Title	North West	North East	South	Midlands	London	Wales	Nothern Ireland	Total Sales	Price	Income
4	War of the Roses	570	340	456	650	420	123	67		12.99	
5	The Deathly Hallows	600	200	560	400	390	213	98		10.9	
6	How to be the Best at Everything	435	100	600	809	698	145	78		12	
7	Grow your own Veg	444	321	900	689	765	132	77		23.5	
8	Restless	500	200	450	445	478	121	88		13	
9	Understanding the Weather	234	123	500	456	700	99	100		18.5	
10											

Figure 5.7: Adding all the numbers to your worksheet.

Formatting text

To make a spreadsheet easier to understand, it is worth formatting it to break up the block of numbers. The easiest way to do this is to add borders to the column and rows but you can also change the text size, font, alignment, whether or not it is bold or italic, colour, etc. The activity below guides you through how to do this.

Activity 2: Formatting text...

In this activity you will:

● format the text and numbers in your spreadsheet.

▶ Open the spreadsheet you have been working on.

The company wants the headings for columns **B** to **K** to be italic and right-aligned.

▶ Click on column **B3**.

▶ While holding the left mouse button down, drag the mouse across to **K3**.

▶ Release the mouse.

You will notice that the cells you wish to change are now highlighted.

	A	B	C	D	E	F	G	H	I	J	K
1	Sales Figures for July										
2											
3	Book Title	North West	North East	South	Midlands	London	Wales	Nothern Ireland	Total Sales	Price	Income
4	War of the Roses	570	340	456	650	420	123	67		12.99	
5	The Deathly Hallows	600	200	560	400	390	213	98		10.9	
6	How to be the Best at Everything	435	100	600	809	698	145	78		12	
7	Grow your own Veg	444	321	900	689	765	132	77		23.5	
8	Restless	500	200	450	445	478	121	88		13	
9	Understanding the Weather	234	123	500	456	700	99	100		18.5	
10											

Figure 5.8: The highlighted column headings.

▶ First click on the **Align Right** button.

▶ Next click on the **Italic** button.

The Align Right button.

The headings in columns **B** to **K** should now be italic and right-aligned

The company now wants the title **Sales Figures for July** to be in bold.

The Italic button.

▶ Click on cell **A1**.

▶ Click on the **Bold** button.

The Bold button.

Finally, the text in cell **A3** should be bold and centred.

▶ Click on cell **A3**.

▶ Click on the **Bold** button.

▶ Click on the **Centre** button.

The Centre button.

▶ Save your work.

▶ Your spreadsheet should now look like the one in Figure 5.9.

	A	B	C	D	E	F	G	H	I	J	K
1	Sales Figures for July										
2											
3	**Book Title**	*North West*	*North East*	*South*	*Midlands*	*London*	*Wales*	*Nothern Ireland*	*Total Sales*	*Price*	*Income*
4	War of the Roses	570	340	456	650	420	123	67		12.99	
5	The Deathly Hallows	600	200	560	400	390	213	98		10.9	
6	How to be the Best at Everything	435	100	600	809	698	145	78		12	
7	Grow your own Veg	444	321	900	689	765	132	77		23.5	
8	Restless	500	200	450	445	478	121	88		13	
9	Understanding the Weather	234	123	500	456	700	99	100		18.5	
10											

Figure 5.9: *The spreadsheet with reformatted headings.*

Adding borders and changing the background

In order to make your column headings stand out, you can add a border to them. You can also add a background colour behind them to make them even more prominent. The activity below will show you how to do this.

Activity 3: Adding borders/changing background colour...

In this activity you will:

● add a border to column headings
● change the background colour.

To add a border around the column headings:

▶ Highlight the cells **A3** to **K3**.

▶ Click the arrow to the right of the **Borders** button.

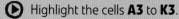

The Borders button.

▶ Click the **Outside Borders** button in the choice of borders.

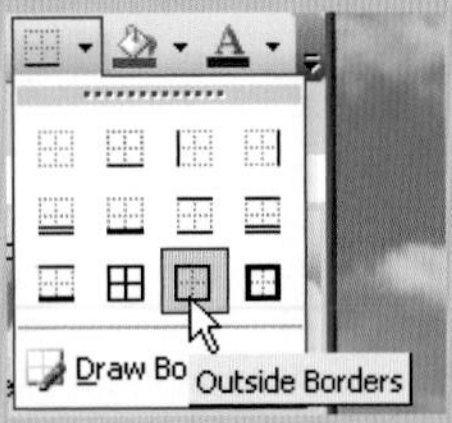

Figure 5.10: The Outside Borders button.

▶ Click outside the highlighted cells on any blank part of your spreadsheet.

▶ Your spreadsheet should look like the one in Figure 5.11.

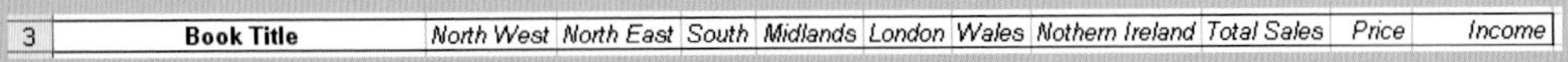

3	**Book Title**	*North West*	*North East*	*South*	*Midlands*	*London*	*Wales*	*Nothern Ireland*	*Total Sales*	*Price*	*Income*

Figure 5.11: A border has been added around the column headings.

To change the background colour:

▶ Highlight the cells **A3** to **K3**.

▶ Click the **Fill Color** button.

▶ Click outside the highlighted cells on any blank part of your spreadsheet.

The Fill Color button.

▶ Your spreadsheet should look like the one in Figure 5.12.

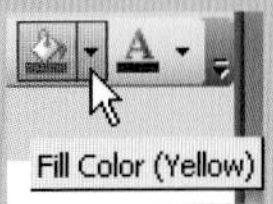

3	**Book Title**	*North West*	*North East*	*South*	*Midlands*	*London*	*Wales*	*Nothern Ireland*	*Total Sales*	*Price*	*Income*

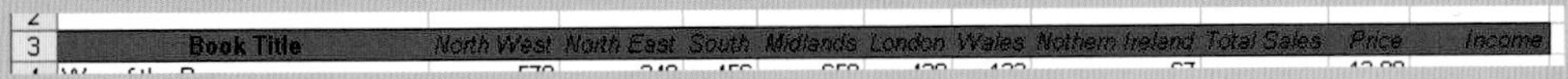

Figure 5.12: The background colour has been added to the column headings.

Formatting numbers in a spreadsheet

Sometimes you need to format numbers in a spreadsheet so that it makes more sense and shows exactly what the numbers represent, for example, currency, percentages or fractions, etc. In the activity below, you are going to format two columns of numbers so that they represent money, set to 2 decimal places so that it shows pounds and pence.

Activity 4: Formatting numbers...

In this activity you will:

● format numbers to show currency.

The price of the books shown in column **J** and the total income shown in column **K** need to be shown as currency.

We will start with column **J** so that the numbers are displayed with a currency symbol and 2 decimal places.

▶ Open the spreadsheet called **Book Sales Figures**.

▶ Highlight Cells **J4** to **J9**.

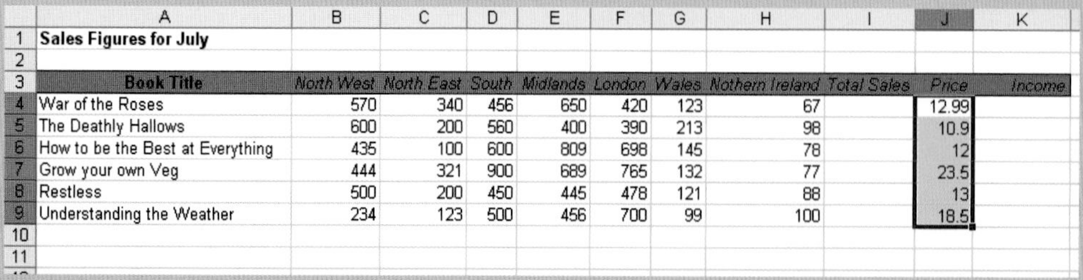

	A	B	C	D	E	F	G	H	I	J	K
1	Sales Figures for July										
2											
3	Book Title	North West	North East	South	Midlands	London	Wales	Nothern Ireland	Total Sales	Price	Income
4	War of the Roses	570	340	456	650	420	123	67		12.99	
5	The Deathly Hallows	600	200	560	400	390	213	98		10.9	
6	How to be the Best at Everything	435	100	600	809	698	145	78		12	
7	Grow your own Veg	444	321	900	689	765	132	77		23.5	
8	Restless	500	200	450	445	478	121	88		13	
9	Understanding the Weather	234	123	500	456	700	99	100		18.5	
10											
11											

Figure 5.13: *Column J highlighted.*

▶ Click **Format**, then **Cells** on the menu bar.

▶ The **Format Cells** dialogue box will be displayed.

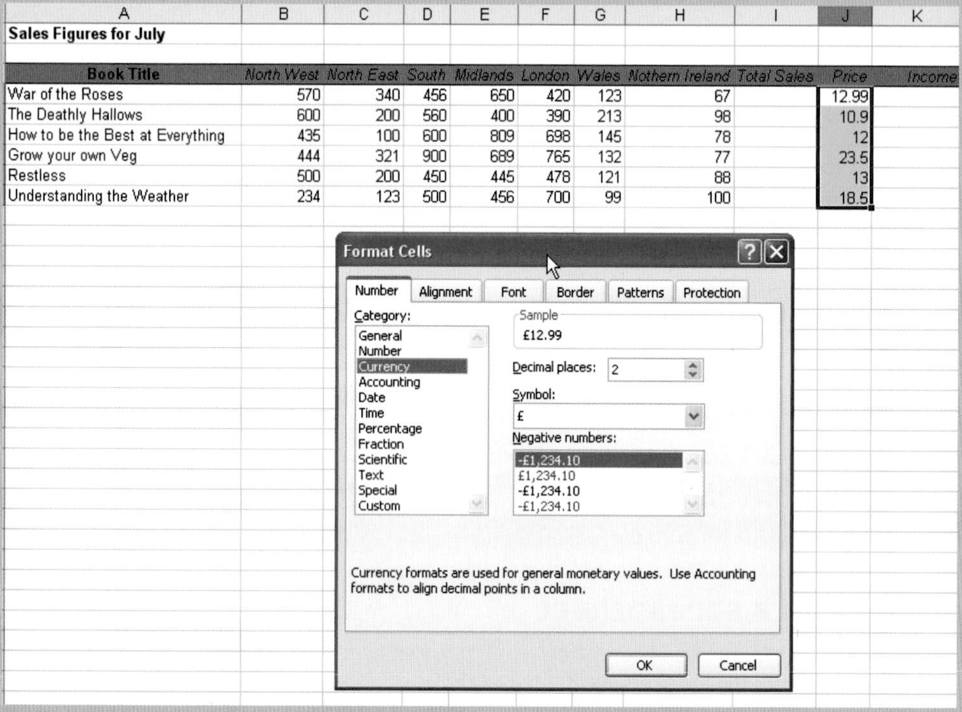

	A	B	C	D	E	F	G	H	I	J	K
	Sales Figures for July										
	Book Title	North West	North East	South	Midlands	London	Wales	Nothern Ireland	Total Sales	Price	Income
	War of the Roses	570	340	456	650	420	123	67		12.99	
	The Deathly Hallows	600	200	560	400	390	213	98		10.9	
	How to be the Best at Everything	435	100	600	809	698	145	78		12	
	Grow your own Veg	444	321	900	689	765	132	77		23.5	
	Restless	500	200	450	445	478	121	88		13	
	Understanding the Weather	234	123	500	456	700	99	100		18.5	

Format Cells

Number | Alignment | Font | Border | Patterns | Protection

Category:
General
Number
Currency
Accounting
Date
Time
Percentage
Fraction
Scientific
Text
Special
Custom

Sample: £12.99

Decimal places: 2

Symbol: £

Negative numbers:
-£1,234.10
£1,234.10
-£1,234.10
-£1,234.10

Currency formats are used for general monetary values. Use Accounting formats to align decimal points in a column.

OK | Cancel

Figure 5.14: *The Format Cells dialogue box.*

▶ Click the **Number tab** if it isn't already selected and then choose **Currency** in the category list.

▶ Make sure the number in the box next to the decimal places is set to **2**.

▶ Make sure the symbol is shown as a **£** sign. If it is not, click the down arrow on the right side of the box and choose the **£** symbol from the options given.

▶ Click **OK**.

▶ Format **K4** to **K9** in the same way to show UK currency to 2 decimal places.

▶ Save your spreadsheet.

Entering formulas

Formulas entered into cells are used to perform calculations based on numbers in other cells. For example, you might want to add up all the numbers in a column and show the total in a separate cell at the bottom of the column. The cell that holds the total of the calculation will contain a formula (that you have entered) to allow it to do this. The most common graphical symbols that you will use in a spreadsheet formula are:

+	To add
–	To subtract
/	To divide
*	To multiply
=	Use at the start of a formula

Activity 5: Inserting and replicating (copying) formulas...

In this activity you will:

- insert and replicate formulas
- use the AutoSum function
- use the Average function.

First you need to insert a formula in row 4 which adds up the total sales for the whole of the UK for the book War of the Roses.

 Click in cell **I4**, then click the **AutoSum** button on the toolbar.

You will notice that the software automatically outlines cells **B4** to **H4** and the formula = SUM(B4:H4) will be displayed in cell **I4**.

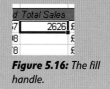

The AutoSum button.

	A	B	C	D	E	F	G	H	I	J	K
1	Sales Figures for July										
2											
3	**Book Title**	North West	North East	South	Midlands	London	Wales	Nothern Ireland	Total Sales	Price	Income
4	War of the Roses	570	340	456	650	420	123	67	B4:H4		
5	The Deathly Hallows	600	200	560	400	390	213	98	SUM(**number1**, [number2], ...)		
6	How to be the Best at Everything	435	100	600	809	698	145	78		£12.00	
7	Grow your own Veg	444	321	900	689	765	132	77		£23.50	
8	Restless	500	200	450	445	478	121	88		£13.00	
9	Understanding the Weather	234	123	500	456	700	99	100		£18.50	
10											

SUM ▾ ✗ ✓ ƒx =SUM(B4:H4)

Figure 5.15: Carrying out an auto calculation.

▶ Press **Enter**.

You now need to copy or replicate the formula down from **I4** to **I9** so that it will calculate the sales of all books.

▶ Click in cell **I4**. You will see a small black square in the bottom right-hand corner. This is called a fill handle.

d Total Sales	
7	2626 £
8	£
8	£

Figure 5.16: The fill handle.

Figure 5.17: *The autofill cross.*

- ▶ Move the mouse pointer over the fill handle and you will notice it changes into a thin, black cross.

- ▶ Click and hold the left mouse button and drag your mouse down as far as column **I9**.

- ▶ The formula will have been replicated in the other cells and your spreadsheet should now look like Figure 5.18 below.

	A	B	C	D	E	F	G	H	I	J	K
1	Sales Figures for July										
2											
3	Book Title	North West	North East	South	Midlands	London	Wales	Nothern Ireland	Total Sales	Price	Income
4	War of the Roses	570	340	456	650	420	123	67	2626	£12.99	
5	The Deathly Hallows	600	200	560	400	390	213	98	2461	£10.90	
6	How to be the Best at Everything	435	100	600	809	698	145	78	2865	£12.00	
7	Grow your own Veg	444	321	900	689	765	132	77	3328	£23.50	
8	Restless	500	200	450	445	478	121	88	2282	£13.00	
9	Understanding the Weather	234	123	500	456	700	99	100	2212	£18.50	
10											
11											

Figure 5.18: *The formula in I4 has been replicated, calculating the total sales for each book.*

You now need to add the income for each book by multiplying the price by the total sales.

- ▶ Click cell **K4** and enter the following formula:

    =J4*I4

- ▶ Press **Enter**.

- ▶ Click back on cell **K4**.

- ▶ Move the pointer over the fill handle until it turns into a thin black cross.

- ▶ Drag down to cell **K9**.

- ▶ Save your spreadsheet.

> ⊕**TIP**
>
> As well as dragging your cursor down the cell range, you can also just simply type in the cell range making sure you use the : symbol in between your first and last cell reference.

Your spreadsheet should now look like the one in Figure 5.19.

	A	B	C	D	E	F	G	H	I	J	K	L
1	Sales Figures for July											
2												
3	Book Title	North West	North East	South	Midlands	London	Wales	Nothern Ireland	Total Sales	Price	Income	
4	War of the Roses	570	340	456	650	420	123	67	2626	£12.99	£34,111.74	
5	The Deathly Hallows	600	200	560	400	390	213	98	2461	£10.90	£26,824.90	
6	How to be the Best at Everything	435	100	600	809	698	145	78	2865	£12.00	£34,380.00	
7	Grow your own Veg	444	321	900	689	765	132	77	3328	£23.50	£78,208.00	
8	Restless	500	200	450	445	478	121	88	2282	£13.00	£29,666.00	
9	Understanding the Weather	234	123	500	456	700	99	100	2212	£18.50	£40,922.00	
10												
11												

Figure 5.19: *The formula in K4 has been replicated, calculating the total income for each book.*

> ⊕**TIP**
>
> If you need to duplicate your calculations, i.e. copy the values of each cell into another worksheet, using the Cut, Copy and Paste commands in your spreadsheet software, you can move or copy entire cells or their contents. For example, you can copy the value of a formula without copying the formula itself, or you can copy only the formula by using the Paste Options symbol that appears when you have pasted your cells into their new location.

The company would like to know which region has sold the most books. To calculate this information, you will need to add totals in row 10.

▶ Click on cell **B10**.

▶ Add the formula:

> **=SUM(B4:B9)**

▶ Press **Enter**.

▶ Click on cell **B10**.

▶ Drag the cursor across to **I10**.

▶ Press **Enter**.

Your spreadsheet should now look like the one in Figure 5.20.

	A	B	C	D	E	F	G	H	I	J	K
1	Sales Figures for July										
2											
3	Book Title	North West	North East	South	Midlands	London	Wales	Nothern Ireland	Total Sales	Price	Income
4	War of the Roses	570	340	456	650	420	123	67	2626	£12.99	£34,111.74
5	The Deathly Hallows	600	200	560	400	390	213	98	2461	£10.90	£26,824.90
6	How to be the Best at Everything	435	100	600	809	698	145	78	2865	£12.00	£34,380.00
7	Grow your own Veg	444	321	900	689	765	132	77	3328	£23.50	£78,208.00
8	Restless	500	200	450	445	478	121	88	2282	£13.00	£29,666.00
9	Understanding the Weather	234	123	500	456	700	99	100	2212	£18.50	£40,922.00
10		2783	1284	3466	3449	3451	833	508	15774		
11											
12											
13											

Figure 5.20: *The formula in B10 has been replicated, calculating the total sales for each region.*

The company would also like to know the total income from sales.

▶ Click on cell **K10**.

▶ Add the formula: **=SUM(K4:K9)**.

▶ Press **Enter**.

▶ Format the cell to show UK currency.

▶ Save the spreadsheet.

Your spreadsheet should now look like the one in Figure 5.21.

	A	B	C	D	E	F	G	H	I	J	K
1	Sales Figures for July										
2											
3	Book Title	North West	North East	South	Midlands	London	Wales	Nothern Ireland	Total Sales	Price	Income
4	War of the Roses	570	340	456	650	420	123	67	2626	£12.99	£34,111.74
5	The Deathly Hallows	600	200	560	400	390	213	98	2461	£10.90	£26,824.90
6	How to be the Best at Everything	435	100	600	809	698	145	78	2865	£12.00	£34,380.00
7	Grow your own Veg	444	321	900	689	765	132	77	3328	£23.50	£78,208.00
8	Restless	500	200	450	445	478	121	88	2282	£13.00	£29,666.00
9	Understanding the Weather	234	123	500	456	700	99	100	2212	£18.50	£40,922.00
10		2783	1284	3466	3449	3451	833	508	15774		£244,112.64
11											
12											
13											

Figure 5.21: *The total income from sales has been calculated in cell K10.*

We have calculated the exact total sales figures above but sometimes it's useful to know the average because it's difficult to remember a whole list of numbers. So here we need to calculate the average of the group of numbers in column **K** which will show us the average income from all of the books sold.

 Select cell **K11**.

 Click the arrow next to **AutoSum** on the toolbar and then click **Average** from the drop-down menu that appears.

 Click **Enter**.

 The average of the cells **K4:K9** will appear in cell **K10**.

H	I	J	K
Northern Ireland	Total Sales	Price	Income
67	2626	£12.99	£34,111.74
98	2461	£10.99	£27,046.39
78	2865	£12.00	£34,380.00
77	3328	£23.50	£78,208.00
88	2282	£13.00	£29,666.00
100	2212	£18.50	£40,922.00
508	15774		£244,334.13
		Average:	£69,809.75

Figure 5.22: *The average of cells J4 to J9 appears in cell J10.*

To make it clear that the figure in K11 is an average it is good practice to add a label.

 Click on cell J11 and type Average:

 Press enter.

 You may need to change the width of column J so that the text fits.

 Right-align the text in cell J11.

Inserting columns into a spreadsheet

Sometimes you will find that you need to add an extra column into your spreadsheet, in order to enter extra information. The activity below shows you how to do this without upsetting the formulas you have already entered.

Activity 6: Inserting a column...

In this activity you will:

- insert a column into a spreadsheet.

When the spreadsheet was produced, sales figures in Scotland were missed off the list. You now need to add a column to show the sales figures for the books sold in Scotland.

 Open the spreadsheet you have been working on above.

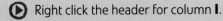

- ▶ Right click the header for column **I**.

- ▶ Select **Insert**.

- ▶ A new column will appear.

- ▶ Click in cell **I3**.

- ▶ Type in **Scotland**.

- ▶ Add the sales figures as shown below in column **I** – you will notice that total sales and income will change as you enter the numbers.

	A	B	C	D	E	F	G	H	I	J	K	L
1	Sales Figures for July											
2												
3	Book Title	North West	North East	South	Midlands	London	Wales	Northern Ireland	Scotland	Total Sales	Price	Income
4	War of the Roses	570	340	456	650	420	123	67	233	2859	£12.99	£37,138.41
5	The Deathly Hallo	600	200	560	400	390	213	98	122	2583	£10.99	£28,387.17
6	How to be the Be	435	100	600	809	698	145	78	134	2999	£12.00	£35,988.00
7	Grow your own V	444	321	900	689	765	132	77	213	3541	£23.50	£83,213.50
8	Restless	500	200	450	445	478	121	88	122	2404	£13.00	£31,252.00
9	Understanding th	234	123	500	456	700	99	100	11	2223	£18.50	£41,125.50
10		2783	1284	3466	3449	3451	833	508		16609		£257,104.58
11											Average:	£73,458.45
12												

Figure 5.23: *A new column has been inserted for Scotland and its sales figures.*

- ▶ Click on cell **H10**.

- ▶ Right click on the mouse.

- ▶ Select **Copy** from the drop-down menu.

	A	B	C	D	E	F	G	H	I	J
1	Sales Figures for July									
2										
3	Book Title	North West	North East	South	Midlands	London	Wales	Northern Ireland	Scotland	Total Sales
4	War of the Roses	570	340	456	650	420	123	67	233	2859
5	The Deathly Hallo	600	200	560	400	390	213	98	122	2583
6	How to be the Be	435	100	600	809	698	145	78	134	2999
7	Grow your own V	444	321	900	689	765	132	77	213	3541
8	Restless	500	200	450	445	478	121	88	122	2404
9	Understanding th	234	123	500	456	700	99	100	11	2223
10		2783	1284	3466	3449	3451	833	508		16609
11										
12										
13										
14										
15										
16										
17										
18										
19										
20										
21										
22										
23										
24										
25										
26										
27										
28										
29										
30										

Context menu:
- ✂ Cut
- 📋 Copy
- 📋 Paste
- Paste Special...
- Insert...
- Delete...
- Clear Contents
- Insert Comment
- Format Cells...
- Pick From Drop-down List...
- Add Watch
- Create List...
- Hyperlink...
- Look Up...

Figure 5.24: *Select Copy from the drop-down menu.*

Click on cell **I10**.

 Right click on the mouse.

 Select **Paste**.

	A	B	C	D	E	F	G	H		I	J	K	L
1	Sales Figures for July												
2													
3	Book Title	North West	North East	South	Midlands	London	Wales	Northern Ireland		Scotland	Total Sales	Price	Income
4	War of the Roses	570	340	456	650	420	123	67		233	2859	£12.99	£37,138.41
5	The Deathly Hallows	600	200	560	400	390	213	98		122	2583	£10.99	£28,387.17
6	How to be the Best at Everything	435	100	600	809	698	145	78		134	2999	£12.00	£35,988.00
7	Grow your own Veg	444	321	900	689	765	132	77		213	3541	£23.50	£83,213.50
8	Restless	500	200	450	445	478	121	88		122	2404	£13.00	£31,252.00
9	Understanding the Weather	234	123	500	456	700	99	100		11	2223	£18.50	£41,125.50
10		2783	1284	3466	3449	3451	833	508			16609		£257,104.58
11													3,458.45

Right-click menu:
- Cut
- Copy
- Paste
- Paste Special...
- Insert...
- Delete...
- Clear Contents
- Insert Comment
- Format Cells...
- Pick From Drop-down List...
- Add Watch
- Create List...
- Hyperlink...
- Look Up...

Figure 5.25 *Select Paste from the drop-down menu.*

You will notice that the formula has been copied from cell **H10** to cell **I10** and the cell references have automatically changed to add the total sales for Scotland.

 Save your spreadsheet.

An error has been noticed in cell **E7**.

 Select cell **E7**.

 Type the value **724** into the cell.

The values in cells **J10** and **L10** have changed automatically.

Another book needs to be added to the list.

 Click on **Row 8** to select the row.

 Select **Insert, Row** from the menu bar.

Insert | Format | Tools | D
- Cells
- Rows
- Columns
- Worksheet
- Chart...
- Symbol...

Figure 5.26: *Insert row.*

A new row will appear above **Row 8**.

	A	B	C	D	E	F
1	**Sales Figures for July**					
2						
3	*Book Title*	*North West*	*North East*	*South*	*Midlands*	*London*
4	War of the Roses	570	340	456	650	420
5	The Deathly Hallows	600	200	560	400	390
6	How to be the Best at Everything	435	100	600	809	698
7	Grow your own Veg	444	321	900	724	765
8						
9	Restless	500	200	450	445	478
10	Understanding the Weather	234	123	500	456	700
11		2783	1284	3466	3484	3451

Figure 5.27: *The inserted row.*

▶ Add the data shown below:

Children's Toys	258	645	225	369	514	712	27	125

The **Total Sales** figures and Income has been automatically updated.

▶ Click on **Row 8** to select the row.

▶ Select **Edit, Delete** from the menu bar.

Edit	View	Insert	Form
↶	Can't Undo	Ctrl+Z	
✄	Cut	Ctrl+X	
▤	Copy	Ctrl+C	
📋	Paste	Ctrl+V	
	Paste Special...		
	Clear	▶	
	Delete		
	Delete Sheet		
🔍	Find...	Ctrl+F	
	⌄		

Figure 5.28: *Delete row.*

Row 8 will be removed.

▶ Select cell **A15**. Type **Average Book Sales by Area**.

▶ Select cell **B15**. Type in the following formula: **=(B4+B5+B6+B7+B8+B9)/6**.

The average book sales will appear in cell B15.

A	B	
Sales Figures for July		
Book Title	*North West*	*N*
War of the Roses	570	
The Deathly Hallows	600	
How to be the Best at Everything	435	
Grow your own Veg	444	
Restless	500	
Understanding the Weather	234	
	2783	
Average Book Sales by Area	463.83	

Figure 5.29: *Average Sales.*

 Select cell **A15** again.

 Type **Percentage Book Sales by Area**.

 Select cell **B15**. Type in the following formula **=SUM(B4:B9)/J10**.

 Format the cell **B15** by selecting **Format, Cells** from the menu bar.

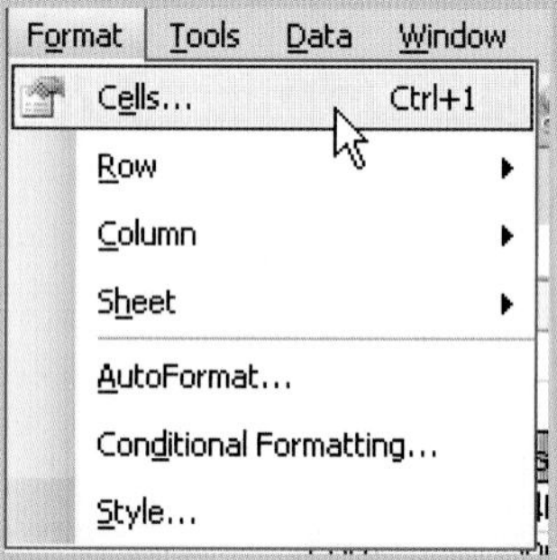

Format	Tools	Data	Window
Cells...			Ctrl+1
Row			▶
Column			▶
Sheet			▶
AutoFormat...			
Conditional Formatting...			
Style...			

Figure 5.30: *Format cells.*

 Select the **Number tab**.

 Select **Percentage** from the category list.

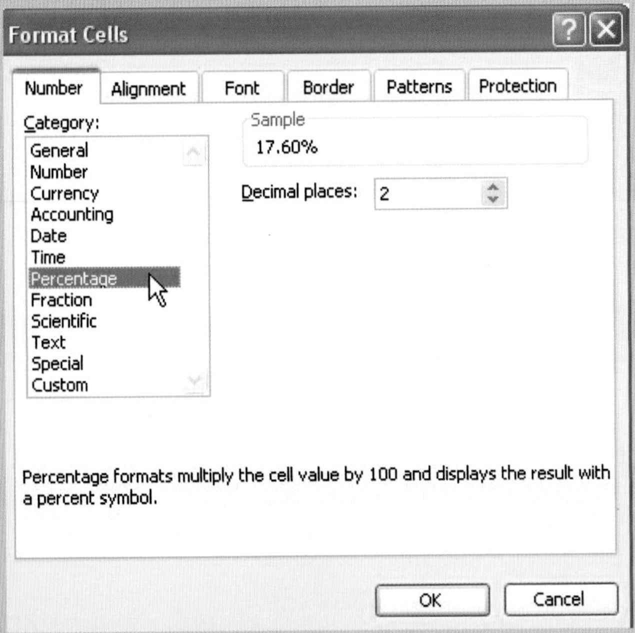

Figure 5.31: Format number.

▶ Click **OK** to apply the formatting.

▶ Save your work.

Showing/hiding formulas

In order to gain **Pass**, **Merit** or **Distinction**, you need to be able to show and print out any formulas and functions that you have used in your spreadsheet.

Activity 7: Showing/hiding formulas...

In this activity you will:

- display and hide the formulas in your spreadsheet.

▶ Go to the **Tools** menu and click on **Options** from the drop-down menu. The options dialogue box will appear.

▶ Click the **View** tab and then, in the **Windows Options** section, tick the box next to **Formulas**.

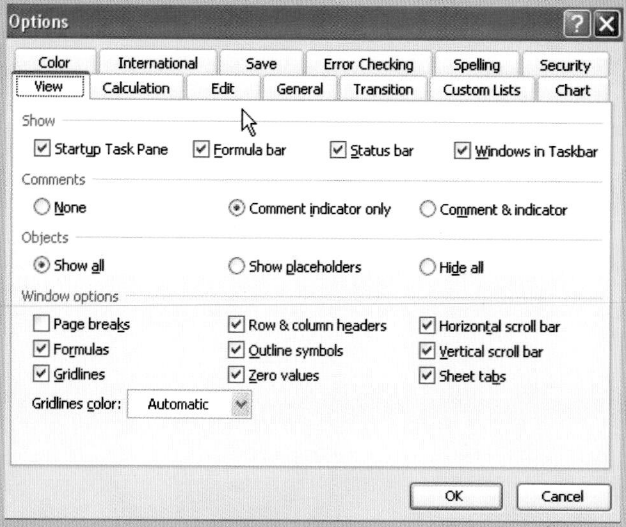

Figure 5.32: *The Options dialogue box.*

▶ Click **OK**.

▶ The formulas will now appear in your spreadsheet.

To hide the formulas again, un-tick the **Formulas** box.

Printing a spreadsheet

In order to achieve any of the grading criteria, you must be able to print out your spread-sheet. The activity below shows you how to add gridlines to your spreadsheet prior to printing. You'll also discover how you can make your spreadsheet fit onto one page.

Activity 8: Printing a spreadsheet...

In this activity you will:

- use the **Page Setup** function to fit your spreadsheet onto one page for printing
- print a spreadsheet showing formulas
- print a spreadsheet showing gridlines.

▶ Open your spreadsheet.

▶ Click **File** on the menu bar.

▶ Select **Page Setup**.

▶ The **Page Setup** dialogue box will appear.

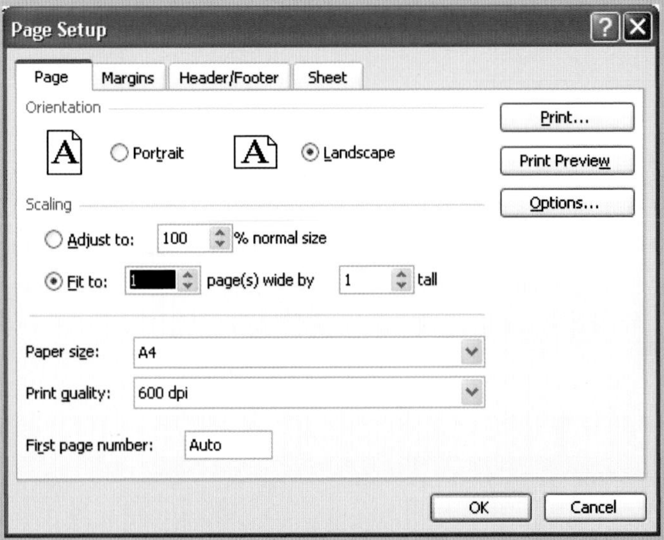

Figure 5.33: *The Page Setup dialogue box.*

▶ Click on the **Page** tab.

▶ Select the radio button next to **Landscape** by clicking on it.

▶ In the scaling section, click on the **Fit to** radio button.

You should leave the other option as 1 page wide by 1 tall.

▶ Click on the **Sheet tab**.

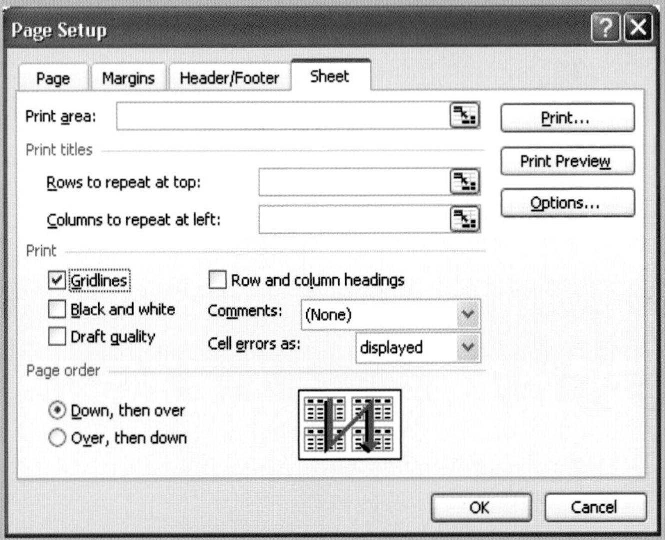

Figure 5.34: *The Page Setup options.*

▶ In the **Print** section, tick the **Gridlines** box.

▶ Click **Print Preview**.

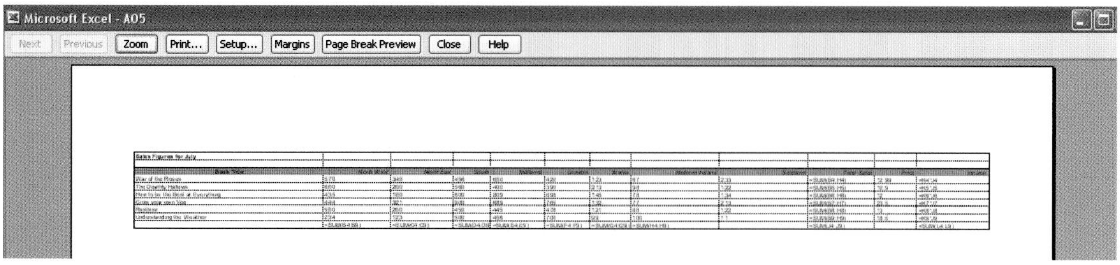

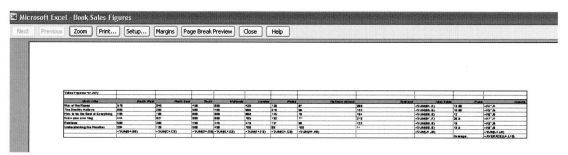

Figure 5.35: *Your spreadsheet in Print Preview.*

To make sure your printed spreadsheet shows formulas:

▶ Close the print preview screen.

▶ Go to the **Tools** menu and click on **Options** from the drop-down menu.

▶ Click the **View** tab and then, in the **Windows Options** section, tick the box next to **Formulas**.

▶ Click **OK**, then click **Print Preview**.

Your spreadsheet will be displayed exactly as it will be printed. It should look like Figure 5.36 below.

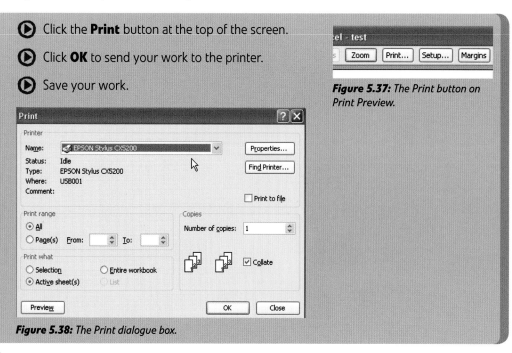

Figure 5.36: *Your spreadsheet showing formulas in Print Preview.*

▶ Click the **Print** button at the top of the screen.

▶ Click **OK** to send your work to the printer.

▶ Save your work.

Figure 5.37: *The Print button on Print Preview.*

Figure 5.38: *The Print dialogue box.*

Headers and footers

You can add headers and footers to your spreadsheets to display a variety of information including the date, time and page number – you can even add a picture to a header or footer such as the company logo. This is very useful especially for large documents, to ensure that you have all of the relevant pages and in the correct order. The activity below shows you how to add a date and a page number to your spreadsheet.

Activity 9: Entering information into a header or footer...

In this activity you will:

* add information into the header and footer sections of your spreadsheet
* print out your work showing headers and footers.

▶ Click **View** on the menu bar and scroll down the menu to **Header and Footer**.

▶ Click **Header and Footer**. The **Page Setup** box will appear.

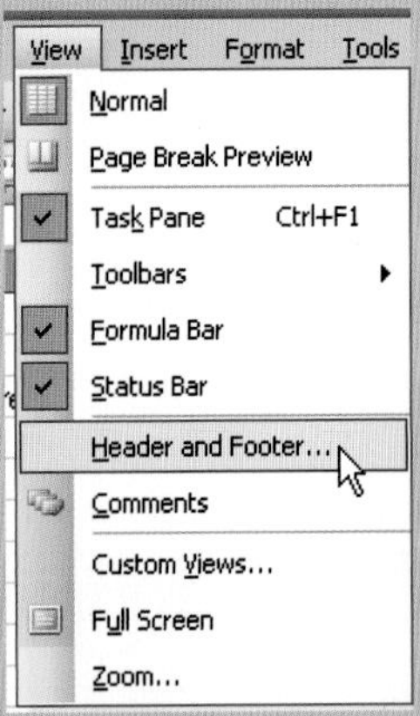

Figure 5.39: *Selecting Header and Footer from the View drop-down menu.*

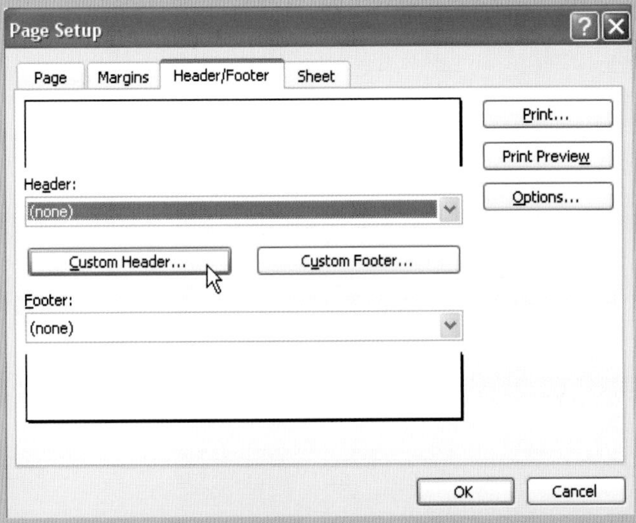

Figure 5.40: *The Page Setup dialogue box and the Custom Header button.*

▶ Click **Custom Header**.

▶ Click in the **Left section** box.

▶ On the row of buttons in the **Header** dialogue box, click **Date**.

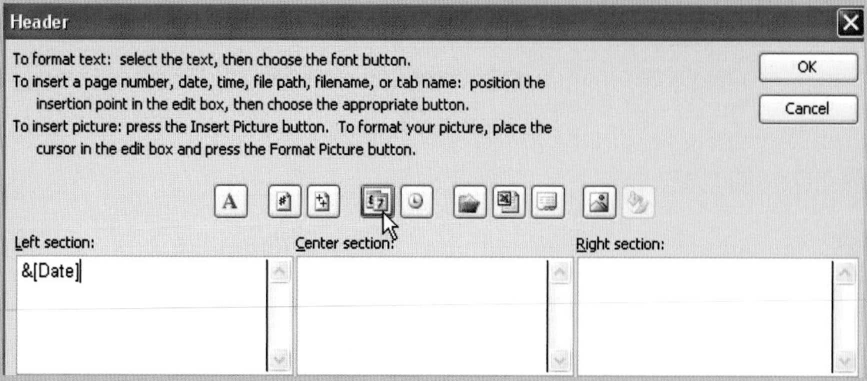

Header   ☒

To format text: select the text, then choose the font button.   OK
To insert a page number, date, time, file path, filename, or tab name: position the
  insertion point in the edit box, then choose the appropriate button.   Cancel
To insert picture: press the Insert Picture button. To format your picture, place the
  cursor in the edit box and press the Format Picture button.

| A | | | | | | | | | |

Left section: **Center section:**   **Right section:**

&[Date]

Figure 5.41: The Date button in the Header dialogue box.

▶ Click **OK** to return to the **Page Setup**.

▶ Your **Page Setup** should look similar to the one in Figure 5.42.

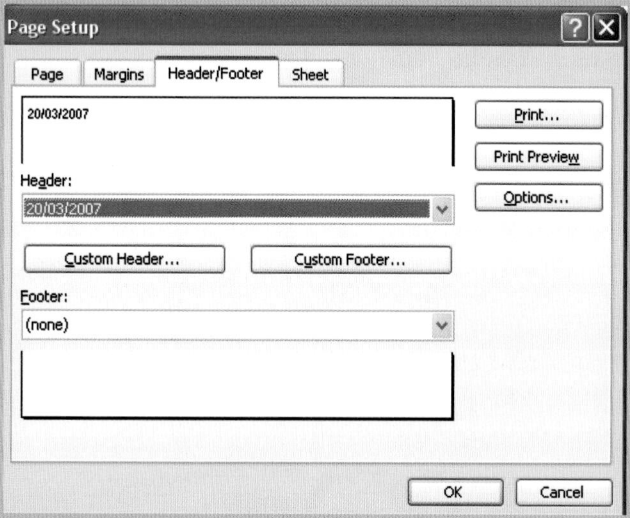

Page Setup   ？☒

| Page | Margins | Header/Footer | Sheet |

20/03/2007   Print...

                                              Print Preview

Header: Options...
20/03/2007   ⌄

Custom Header...   Custom Footer...

Footer:
(none)   ⌄

                                    OK   Cancel

Figure 5.42: The Header date showing in the Page Setup dialogue box.

▶ Click **OK** to exit.

▶ Repeat the same process as outlined above but, this time, add a page number to
your **Footer** in the **Right** section.

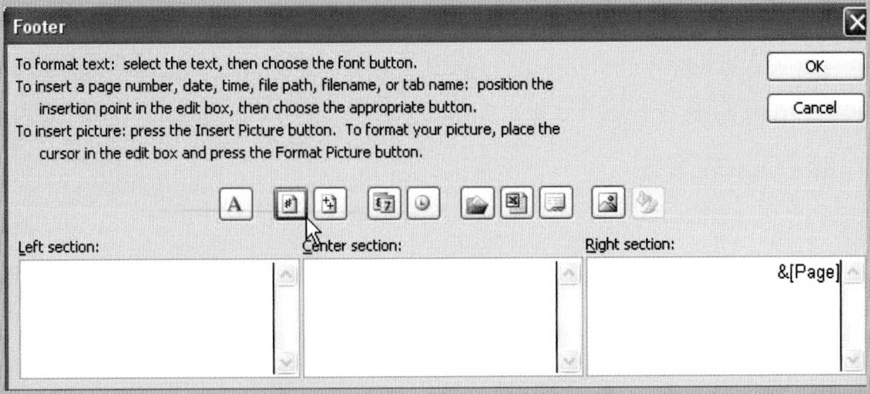

Figure 5.43: *The Page number button in the Footer dialogue box.*

▶ Print out your spreadsheet showing the header and footer.

▶ Save your work.

> **⊕TIP**
>
> To make rows and columns easier to identify in a printout, you can display their headings. Row headings are the row numbers to the left of a worksheet. Column headings are the letters or numbers that appear at the top of the columns on a worksheet.
>
> You can also print column or row labels (or print them as titles) on every page by specifying the rows and columns that you want to repeat at the top or at the left of every printed page.

Portfolio evidence

Based on the topic area that you have chosen in conjunction with your teacher or tutor, use the 'How to achieve' section at the beginning of this chapter to guide you in creating and using your business spreadsheet and including the necessary elements at the level towards which you are working.

The previous sections have given you some indication of how you could go about creating different types of spreadsheets and the types of things that you need to think about when creating them. You should think about:

- creating effective and accurate business spreadsheets
- using different formatting styles to help present your information clearly
- using options within the software to work efficiently
- using a range of formulas
- using a range of print options.

CHAPTER ⑥

→ *Assessment Objective 6*

Using Business Databases

. . . .

Overview:

In this chapter, you will select and use tools and facilities in database software to enter, sort and search for information for business purposes using a realistic business database provided by your centre.

You will also learn how to use an existing database to enter, edit and delete data and the importance of keeping your database up-to-date. You will use the database to sort data and to search for data using more than one criterion. You will also learn how to create and print out reports in different formats.

> In order to complete the activities in this chapter you will need access to an additional file. This file is contained in the Chapter 6 Resources zip file, which can be downloaded from the OCR Nationals in ICT (Units 1 and 21) Student Resources page on the Payne-Gallway website: www.payne-gallway.co.uk.

● **Address Book.mdb**

How this assessment objective will be assessed...

● You will need to use (but do not need to create) a realistic business database.
● For a **Pass,** you will need to provide evidence that you can enter, edit and delete data. You must also show that you can create a simple query. A screenshot could be used to provide this evidence. For a **Merit,** you will provide evidence of your ability to create a report that prints out selected data and that you can sort the database, using a field or range of fields. For a **Distinction,** you must provide evidence of more than one query and proof that you are able to use more than one search criterion. **Distinction** candidates must produce two different types of report.

Skills to use...

You will need to:

● enter, edit and delete data
● sort data
● search for data
● create reports
● print out reports in different formats.

How to achieve...

Pass requirements

P1 You should enter, edit and delete data in a database.

P2 You should create and use at least one simple query, i.e. using a single search criterion.

Merit requirements

M1 You should enter, edit and delete data in a database.

M2 You should create and use at least one simple query, i.e. using a single search criterion, sorting on at least one field.

M3 You should create and use a report to print out selected data for a specific need.

Distinction requirements

D1 You should enter, edit and delete data in a database and will use the data to meet a wide range of business purposes.

D2 You should create and use at least two queries, including more than one criterion, sorting on at least one field.

D3 You should create and use at least two reports to print out selected data in different formats, for example, address labels, table format and list.

Why do we need databases?

We live in a society that collects and stores large amounts of information. A database helps businesses to store, find, organise and report information. Have you ever seen coupons arrive through the post from a supermarket? It's more than likely that these coupons are not the same for everyone the supermarket mails, but that they are tailored to your shopping habits. How do they know what you buy? The information that you provide via loyalty cards is all stored on a database and this helps supermarkets to target their customers individually, making their mailings more meaningful and hopefully getting customers to spend more money or stay loyal to them.

Most businesses, regardless of their size, use databases to store large amounts of information and to keep track of their customers. Some companies can have huge quantities of data to organise. Producing a report from lots of different documents can take a long time – without a computerised database this task would be almost impossible.

Databases are useful to businesses in the following ways:

Business use	Examples
Storing large amounts of data	• Storing customer records • Storing product details • Storing a list of components needed to make a product
Searching for data that meets certain criteria	• Locating a particular customer • Showing how much stock there is left of a particular product • Finding out information about customers
Producing reports	• Producing a sales report • Targeting customers with personalised offers

What is a database?

A database is a tool that allows people to organise and retrieve large amounts of data in a useful format. Databases are really good at managing and manipulating structured information. 'Structured information' can be explained if we consider a telephone directory.

The telephone directory contains several items of information for each person who has a telephone in a particular area: name, address and phone number. The information is written in exactly the same format.

The telephone directory contains a record for each person. The records are sorted alphabetically by the surname field, which is called the key field.

There are three main components to any database application:

• entering or editing data
• storing data
• generating reports.

Computerised databases store the data on the computer's hard drive. The computer can find and process the information much faster than a human brain!

A database can contain a single table of information, such as the telephone directory, or many tables of related information. Each of these tables will be linked to one or more of the other tables, so that you can tie information together to produce reports or to answer questions about the information you have in your database. Multi-file databases are called relational databases; relational databases are made up of two or more tables of information that are connected in some way.

There are two main types of database – a flat file database and a relational database.

Flat file databases

A flat file database stores all the data in a single file and the sorting, searching and printing of reports are all done in this single file.

Flat file databases are:

• easy to use
• suitable for small amounts of data.

Relational databases

In relational databases, the tables of data exist independently. Relational databases use database management systems to link these independent files together.
To create a computer database you need a database program, such as Microsoft Access.

Using the Access database, you will be able to:

- design the structure of your database
- create data entry forms so you can enter information into the database
- validate the data entered and check for inconsistencies
- sort and manipulate the data in the database
- query the database (ask questions about the data)
- produce reports, both on screen and on paper, in a variety of formats.

Note: although Access enables you to carry out the tasks listed above, for the purposes of this Unit you are not required to design the structure of a database, create data entry forms or validate the data entered.

Database terminology

There are five terms that you need to be familiar with and these are: record, field, fieldname, forms and views.

Record

Data is stored in a database in the form of a record.

A record contains all of the information about a single entry. In a telephone book each person listed is considered to be an entry and the details of each entry (surname, first name, address, telephone number) will be contained in their own record.

Records can be sorted in ascending or descending order, alphabetically or numerically.

Field

A field is each single entry within a record, so in our example it would be the actual surname or address of each person, for example, Smith or 15 Torquay Road.

Fieldname

The fieldname is the title of each field within a record, so carrying on our example, the fieldnames would be Surname, First Name, Address and Home Phone, etc.

Forms

Forms are different layouts which are used to enter data or display chosen fields in a database.

Views

In Access there are two important views that you need to use:

- **Design View** – to create a form, you work in Design View. Viewing a form in Design View is like sitting at a workbench surrounded by useful tools.
- **Datasheet View** – in Datasheet view, you can view records in row and column format, so you can see many records at one time. Datasheet View is used for editing existing data. In the activities that follow, you will mainly be working in Datasheet View.

Opening a database

Activity 1: Loading an existing database in Access...

In this activity you will:

- open an existing database in Access.

▶ Load your database software, for example, Microsoft Access.

▶ Go to **File** on the toolbar and click **Open** to find an existing database.

▶ The database you need is called **Address Book**. You should have downloaded this file at the beginning of this unit. Alternatively, your teacher or tutor will tell you where to find this file.

▶ Double click this icon to open the database.

▶ Select **Tables** from the left-hand window by clicking it once.

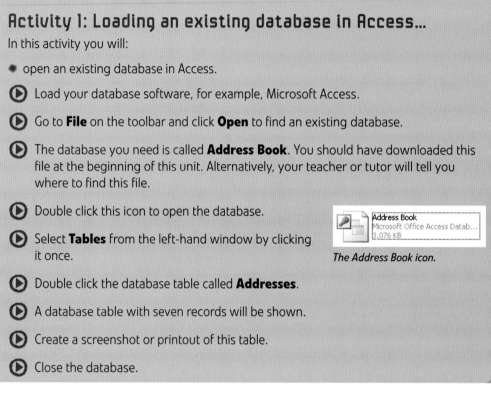

Address Book
Microsoft Office Access Datab...
3,076 KB

The Address Book icon.

▶ Double click the database table called **Addresses**.

▶ A database table with seven records will be shown.

▶ Create a screenshot or printout of this table.

▶ Close the database.

Adding and deleting records

The advantage of taking the time and effort to create a database (with millions of entries in some cases) is that it's very easy to edit them and to keep them up-to-date by adding, deleting or changing records. Imagine having to re-type the phonebook each time somebody moved house! The activity below will show you how to do this.

Activity 2: Adding and deleting records...

In this activity you will:

- add new records
- delete existing records.

There are two ways to add a new record to your database:

▶ Go to **File** on the toolbar and click **Open** to find the database called **Address Book**.

▶ Double click this icon to open the database.

- Make sure **Tables** is selected from the left-hand window.

- Double click on the database called **Addresses**.

Datasheet view is already selected. If you wish to change views:

- Select the drop-down arrow to the right of the datasheet view icon. (See page 118 for a reminder of what 'Datasheet View' means).

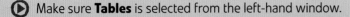

Figure 6.1: Select Datasheet View.

- *Either* click in the blank line at the bottom of the table

- *or* click the **New Record** icon on the toolbar at the top of the screen.

- Enter the new records as shown in Figure 6.2 below.

Addresses

First Name	Last Name	Address	City	Postal Code	Email Address	Home Phone	Mobile Phone	Birthday	Send Card	Nickname
Serena	Ripon	7 Long Road	Bedford	BD8 SR2	serena@example.com	336 98247	77723 65112	17/04/1965	No	Serena
Sanjay	Patel	60 Main Street	Leeds	LD7 SP5	sanjayp@example.co.uk	2254 6932	77756 81435	16/10/1969	No	Sanjay

Figure 6.2: The new records.

Your new database table should look like the one shown in Figure 6.3.

First Name	Last Name	Address	City	Postal Code	Email Address	Home Phone	Mobile Phone	Birthday	Send Card	Nickname
Scott	Fink	12 Hill Drive	London	SW1 8JR	scott@example.com	3598 33654	77725 69554	12/08/1970	No	Scotty
Linda	Mitchell	88 West Lane	London	NW7 LM2	Linda@example.com	1254 66548	77765 15498	04/08/1972	No	Linda
Joe	Cunningham	123 Elm Street	Matlock	MK5 JC4	Joe@example.fr	2155 87456	77745 32654	25/02/1979	Yes	JJ
Mary	Williams	65 North Way	Manchester	MC33 MW5	mary@example.co.uk	3658 26478		17/06/1961	No	Mary
Denise	Smith	27 Green Road	Glasgow	GL5 DS5	denise@example.co.uk	9812 24587	77798 32547	14/07/1975	Yes	Denise
Sally	Cushing	43 Old Oak Road	Birmingham	BM1 SC3	sally@example.co.uk	3487 55423	77723 54871	14/07/1965	Yes	Sally
Serena	Ripon	7 Long Road	Bedford	BD8 SR2	serena@example.com	336 98247	77723 65112	17/04/1965	No	Serena
Sanjay	Patel	60 Main Street	Leeds	LD7 SP5	sanjayp@example.co.uk	2254 6932	77756 81435	16/10/1969	No	Sanjay

Figure 6.3: The completed table.

> (▶) Close the database table by clicking **X** in the top right-hand corner.
>
> (▶) Click **Yes** to save the changes you've just made.

To delete records:

> (▶) Open the **Datasheet View**.
>
> (▶) Click anywhere on the first record in the table.
>
> (▶) Click the **Delete Record** icon on the table **Datasheet** toolbar. A warning message box will appear.

The Delete Record icon.

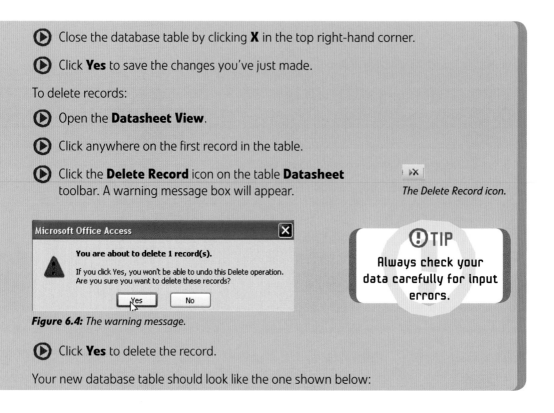

Microsoft Office Access

You are about to delete 1 record(s).

If you click Yes, you won't be able to undo this Delete operation. Are you sure you want to delete these records?

[Yes]   [No]

Figure 6.4: *The warning message.*

> (!) **TIP**
>
> Always check your data carefully for input errors.

> (▶) Click **Yes** to delete the record.

Your new database table should look like the one shown below:

First Name	Last Name	Address	City	Postal Code	Email Address	Home Phone	Mobile Phone	Birthday	Send Card	Nickname
Linda	Mitchell	88 West Lane	London	NW7 LM2	Linda@example.com	1254 66548	77765 15498	04/08/1972	No	Linda
Joe	Cunningham	123 Elm Street	Matlock	MK5 JC4	Joe@example.fr	2155 87456	77745 32654	25/02/1979	Yes	JJ
Mary	Williams	65 North Way	Manchester	MC33 MW5	mary@example.co.uk	3658 26478		17/06/1961	No	Mary
Denise	Smith	27 Green Road	Glasgow	GL5 DS5	denise@example.co.uk	9812 24587	77798 32547	14/07/1975	Yes	Denise
Sally	Cushing	43 Old Oak Road	Birmingham	BM1 SC3	sally@example.co.uk	3487 55423	77723 54871	14/07/1965	Yes	Sally
Serena	Ripon	7 Long Road	Bedford	BD8 SR2	serena@example.com	336 98247	77723 65112	17/04/1965	No	Serena
Sanjay	Patel	60 Main Street	Leeds	LD7 SP5	sanjayp@example.co.uk	2254 6932	77756 81435	16/10/1969	No	Sanjay

Figure 6.5: *The finished database.*

Editing records

The data held in a database can change for many reasons. Changes may involve:

* customer or patient details
* financial data, for example, sales figures
* criminal records.

For instance, your customer might have a new address or it could be that the wrong information has been entered in the first place. In the activity below, a wrong birth date has been entered into a field so it needs to be edited.

Activity 3: Editing records...

In this activity you will:

● edit birthday details in a record.

▶ Open the Access database called **Address Book** in **Datasheet View**.

▶ Select the record for Denise Smith.

▶ Click in the **Birthday** field.

▶ Delete the current birthday using the **Backspace** key.

▶ Type in the new birthday 29/11/1992 and press **Enter**.

The database table should now look like the one shown in Figure 6.6.

First Name	Last Name	Address	City	Postal Code	Email Address	Home Phone	Mobile Phone	Birthday	Send Card	Nickname
Linda	Mitchell	88 West Lane	London	NW7 LM2	Linda@example.com	1254 66548	77765 15498	04/08/1972	No	Linda
Joe	Cunningham	123 Elm Street	Matlock	MK5 JC4	Joe@example.fr	2155 87456	77745 32654	25/02/1979	Yes	JJ
Mary	Williams	65 North Way	Manchester	MC33 MW5	mary@example.co.uk	3658 26478		17/06/1961	No	Mary
Denise	Smith	27 Green Road	Glasgow	GL5 DS5	denise@example.co.uk	9812 24587	77798 32547	29/11/1992	Yes	Denise
Sally	Cushing	43 Old Oak Road	Birmingham	BM1 SC3	sally@example.co.uk	3487 55423	77723 54871	14/07/1965	Yes	Sally
Serena	Ripon	7 Long Road	Bedford	BD8 SR2	serena@example.com	336 98247	77723 65112	17/04/1965	No	Serena
Sanjay	Patel	60 Main Street	Leeds	LD7 SP5	sanjayp@example.co.uk	2254 6932	77756 81435	16/10/1969	No	Sanjay

Figure 6.6: *Denise Smith's birthday has been edited.*

▶ Close the **Address book** database by clicking the **X** in the top right-hand corner of the table window.

▶ Click **Yes** to save the changes to your database table.

Queries

A database is a collection of data or facts, which presented without any background, has no meaning. However, when we put data into context to give it meaning, we call this information. The process of getting information out of your database is called querying. This is where you turn the stored data into information. The main purpose of a database is to turn data into information. Data in databases can be queried in any way that suits your needs. Querying lets you pull out only the data you need to perform your task or answer your question. Using queries, you can retrieve, combine, reuse and analyse your data. You can use queries as a source for forms and reports.

You can search a database using one or several criteria, depending on what you want to find out. Your search criteria are what you use to outline or delimit your search, for example, searching for items priced below or less than (<) £50. You've probably searched many databases when looking at items on the Internet without even knowing it.

The most common search criteria are listed below:

Search criteria	Symbol	Description
Equals	=	Finds records matching a specific value
Less than	<	Finds records whose value is less that the specified amount
Greater than	>	Finds records whose value is greater than the specified amount
Not equal to	<> or =/	Finds records whose value is not equal to the specified amount
Less than or equal to	<=	Finds records whose value is less than or equal to the specified amount
Greater than or equal to	>=	Finds records whose value is greater than or equal to the specified amount

⊘ TIP

You can use queries as a source of records for forms, reports and data access pages.

Activity 4: Searching and sorting a database...

In this activity you will:

- create a simple query to find information
- sort the data into alphabetical order of surname
- display only certain fields
- save your query.

▶ Open the database called **Address Book**.

▶ Click **Queries** in the **Database** window.

▶ Select the option **Create query in Design view**. The **Show Table** window will appear.

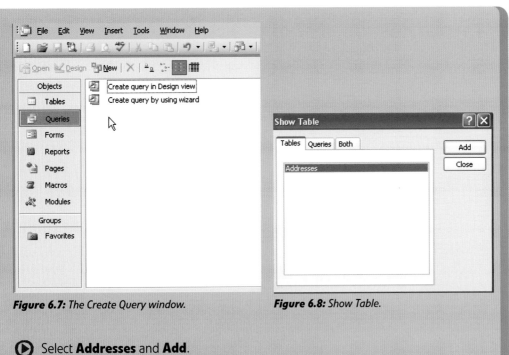

Figure 6.7: *The Create Query window.*

Figure 6.8: *Show Table.*

▶ Select **Addresses** and **Add**.

▶ Click **Close** to close the **Show Table** window.

To select the fields to be displayed:

▶ Double click the fields: **FirstName, LastName, Address, Birthday, SendCard** to add them to the query grid.

Your screen should look like the one in Figure 6.9.

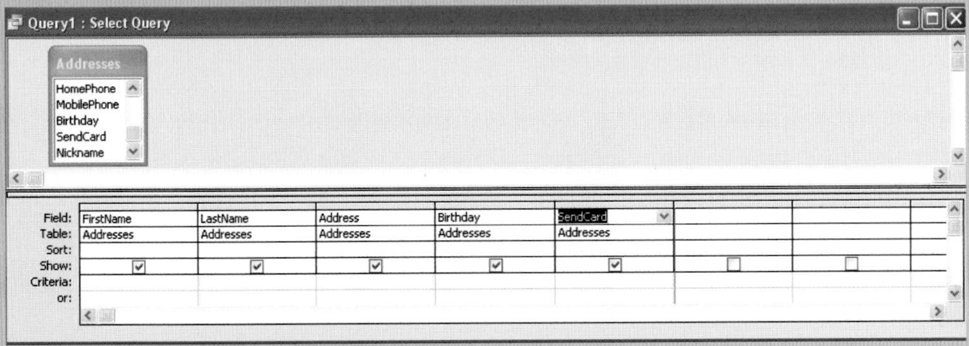

Figure 6.9: *Select Query Fields.*

To sort on a defined field:

▶ Click in the sort row in the **Last Name** column.

▶ Click the arrow and choose **Ascending** from the list of options.

To enter search criteria:

 Click in the **Criteria** row in the **SendCard** column.

 Type **Yes** in the box.

Field:	FirstName	LastName	Address	Birthday	SendCard
Table:	Addresses	Addresses	Addresses	Addresses	Addresses
Sort:		Ascending			
Show:	☑	☑	☑	☑	☑
Criteria:					Yes
or:					

Figure 6.10: *Query and sort criteria.*

 Click the **Run** button on the **Query Design** toolbar.

The Run Query icon.

 Your screen should look like the one shown in Figure 6.11.

Query1 : Select Query

First Name	Last Name	Address	Birthday	Send Card
Joe	Cunningham	123 Elm Street	25/02/1979	Yes
Sally	Cushing	43 Old Oak Road	14/07/1965	Yes
Denise	Smith	27 Green Road	14/07/1975	Yes

Figure 6.11: *Query results.*

To save a query:

 Click **File** on the menu bar.

 Click **Save**.

The file name box will appear.

 Name your query **Send Card**.

 Click **OK**.

Complex queries

It's easy to retrieve data that matches a single search criterion, such as finding all the people to whom you have sent a birthday card.

If you want to match more than one search criterion you will have to use a complex query.

When you design a query you can use the operators AND and OR. A simple search will use only one criterion; a complex search will use more than one criterion (multiple criteria).

Activity 5: Searching a database to find all the records which match more than one criterion...

In this activity you will:

- find all the people in the database with mobile phone numbers and who were also born after 1960
- display selected fields.

▶ Open the database called **Address Book**.

▶ Click **Queries** in the database window.

▶ Double click **Create query in Design view**.

▶ Click **Addresses** and select **Add**.

▶ Click **Close** to close the **Show Table** window.

For this query you will search for all people born after 1960 with a mobile phone number in your address book. You are not going to display the **FirstName** field.

▶ Double click the fields **FirstName, LastName, MobilePhone** and **Birthday** to add them to your query grid.

▶ Click in the **Criteria** row in the **Birthday** column and type **>=1960**.

▶ Click in the **Criteria** row in the **MobilePhone** column and type **NOT "0"**.

To hide the FirstName field:

▶ Click in the **Show** row in the **FirstName** column.

▶ Un-tick the box for this field.

Your screen should look like the one shown in Figure 6.12.

Field:	FirstName	LastName	MobilePhone	Birthday
Table:	Addresses	Addresses	Addresses	Addresses
Sort:				
Show:	☐	☑	☑	☑
Criteria:			Not "0"	>=1960
or:				

Figure 6.12: *The complex query criteria.*

▶ Click the **Run** button on the toolbar to see your results.

Your screen should look like the one in Figure 6.13.

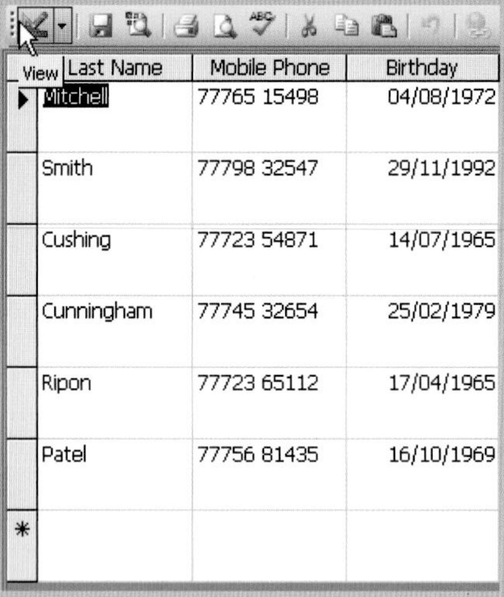

View	Last Name	Mobile Phone	Birthday
▶	Mitchell	77765 15498	04/08/1972
	Smith	77798 32547	29/11/1992
	Cushing	77723 54871	14/07/1965
	Cunningham	77745 32654	25/02/1979
	Ripon	77723 65112	17/04/1965
	Patel	77756 81435	16/10/1969
✳			

Figure 6.13: *The complex query results.*

Creating reports

Reports are a good way to organise and present data from your database. Reports enable you to format your data in an attractive and informative layout for printing or viewing on screen. You can design the output of a report by specifying particular fields to be included. Reports help to structure the output data in specific ways; you can organise data to make it attractive and informative. You can also put the data into alphabetical order or numerical order, for example, the report could list data alphabetically by surname (for example Cushing before Williams).

⊕TIP

You can create a basic report and customise it in Design View to suit your requirements.

Activity 6: Creating a report...

In this activity you will:

● create a report using a wizard
● create address labels.

▶ Open the database called **Address Book**.

▶ Click the **Reports** icon in the left-hand **Database** window.

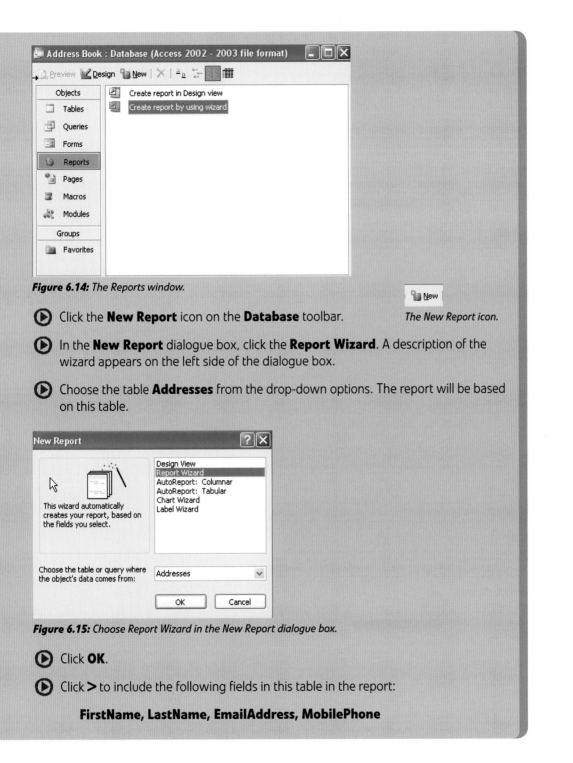

Figure 6.14: *The Reports window.*

▶ Click the **New Report** icon on the **Database** toolbar.

The New Report icon.

▶ In the **New Report** dialogue box, click the **Report Wizard**. A description of the wizard appears on the left side of the dialogue box.

▶ Choose the table **Addresses** from the drop-down options. The report will be based on this table.

Figure 6.15: *Choose Report Wizard in the New Report dialogue box.*

▶ Click **OK**.

▶ Click **>** to include the following fields in this table in the report:

FirstName, LastName, EmailAddress, MobilePhone

Figure 6.16: *Selected Fields in Report Wizard.*

▶ Click **Next**.

▶ Click **Next** (and ignore the grouping levels prompt).

▶ Click **Next** (and ignore the sort order prompt).

▶ Next you need to choose the layout of your report.

▶ Click the radio button for **landscape**.

▶ Click **Next**.

▶ Choose the **Corporate** style from the options given.

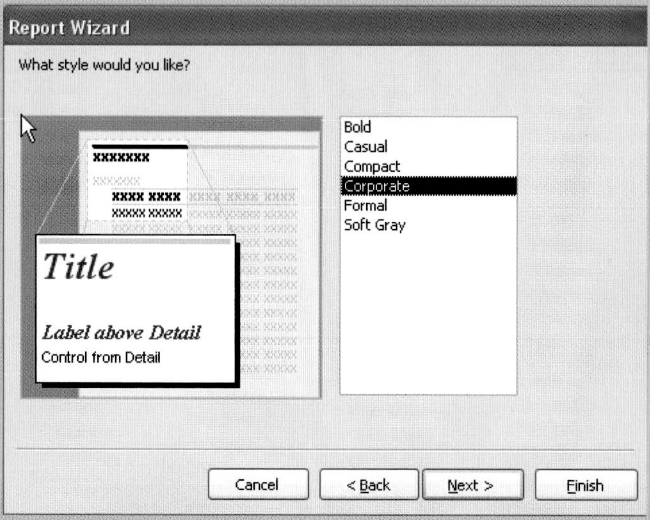

Figure 6.17: *Choose Corporate from the style wizard.*

▶ Click **Next**.

▶ Name your report **My Address Book**.

▶ Click **Finish**.

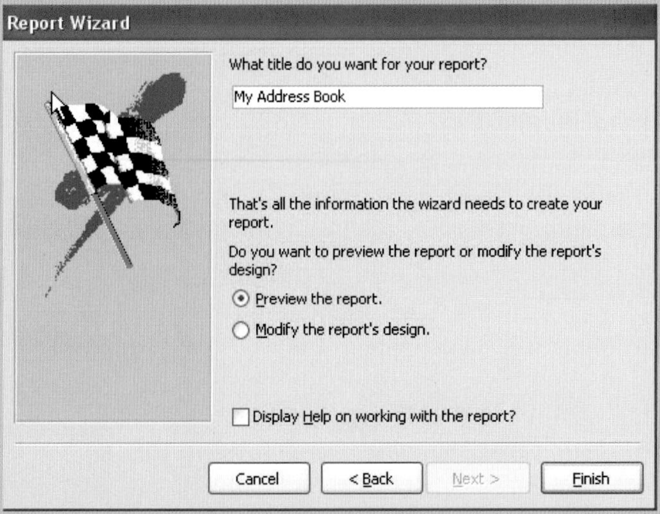

Report Wizard

What title do you want for your report?

My Address Book

That's all the information the wizard needs to create your report.

Do you want to preview the report or modify the report's design?

⦿ Preview the report.

◯ Modify the report's design.

☐ Display Help on working with the report?

| Cancel | < Back | Next > | Finish |

Figure 6.18: Click Finish to end the Report Wizard.

▶ Your report should look like the one in Figure 6.19.

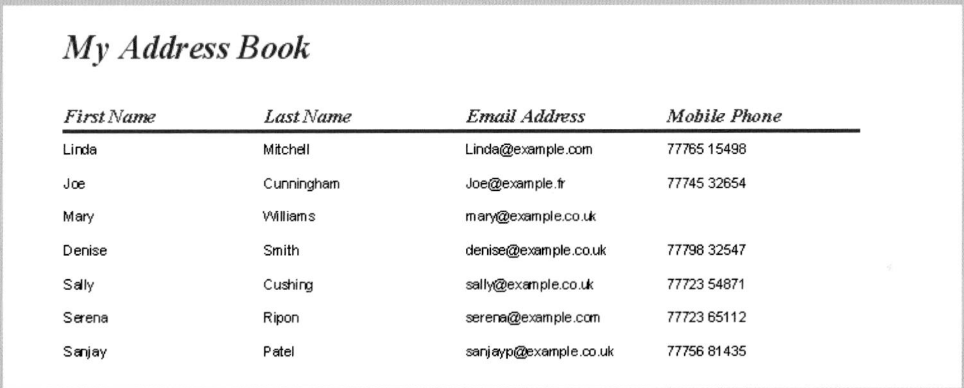

My Address Book

First Name	Last Name	Email Address	Mobile Phone
Linda	Mitchell	Linda@example.com	77765 15498
Joe	Cunningham	Joe@example.fr	77745 32654
Mary	Williams	mary@example.co.uk	
Denise	Smith	denise@example.co.uk	77798 32547
Sally	Cushing	sally@example.co.uk	77723 54871
Serena	Ripon	serena@example.com	77723 65112
Sanjay	Patel	sanjayp@example.co.uk	77756 81435

Figure 6.19: The finished report.

▶ If you find that some of the columns are too narrow to display all the data you can change the column width in the design grid.

▶ Open the query in **Design View**. (You can also resize columns by opening a database table in **Datasheet View**.)

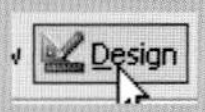

The Design View icon.

▶ Move the pointer to the right edge of the column selector for the column you want to change, until the pointer turns into a two-way arrow.

▶ Drag the edge to the right.

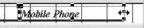

Figure 6.20: The column selector.

▶ Save the changes to your design.

To create address labels:

▶ In the database window, click the **Reports** icon in the left-hand pane.

▶ Click the **New** button on the **Database** toolbar.

▶ In the **New Report** dialogue box, click the **Label Wizard**. A description of the wizard appears on the left side of the dialogue box.

▶ Choose the table **Addresses** from the drop-down options. The report will be based on this table.

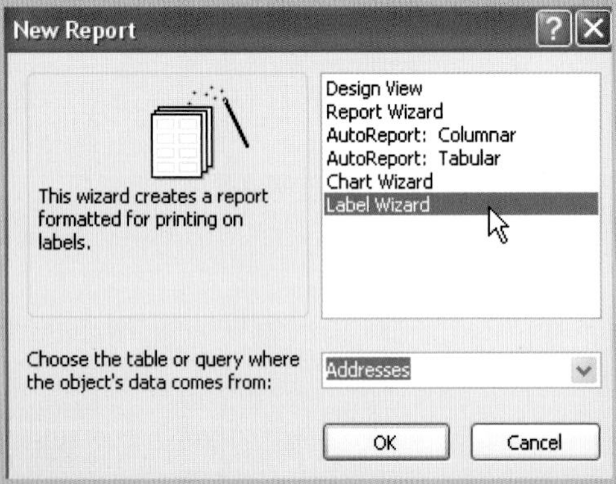

Figure 6.21: Choose Label Wizard in the New Report dialogue box.

▶ Click **OK**.

▶ Click **Next** (and ignore the label size options).

▶ Click **Next** (and ignore the text appearance options).

▶ Choose the following fields from the left box to add to each line of your label:

First Name, Last Name, Address,

City, PostalCode

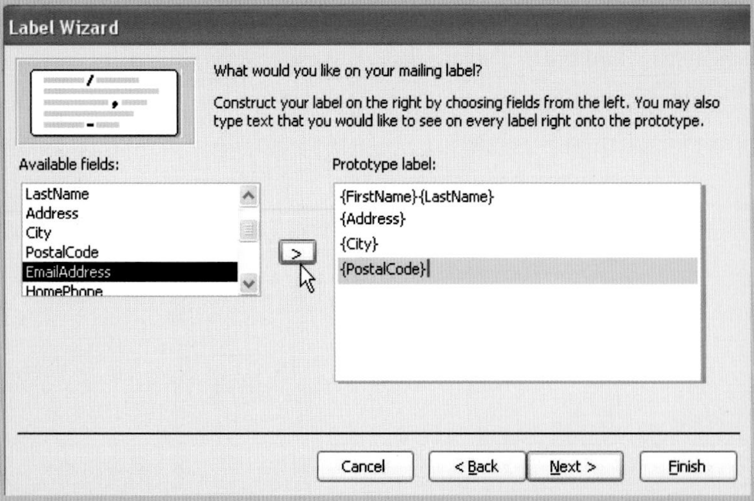

Figure 6.22: Choosing fields for the labels in Label Wizard.

▶ Click **Next** to move to the next window.

▶ Click **Next** (and ignore the sort by: options).

▶ Name your report **My Labels**.

▶ Click **Finish**.

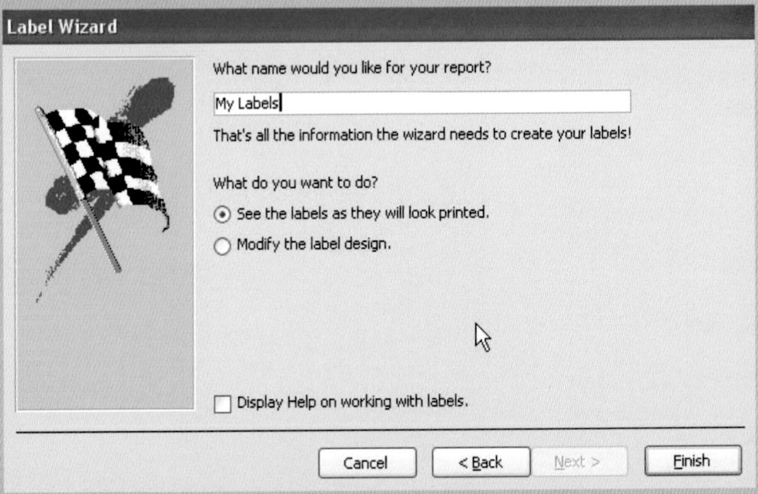

Figure 6.23: *Naming your report My Labels and clicking Finish.*

▶ Click **Finish**.

▶ Your report should look like the one shown in Figure 6.24.

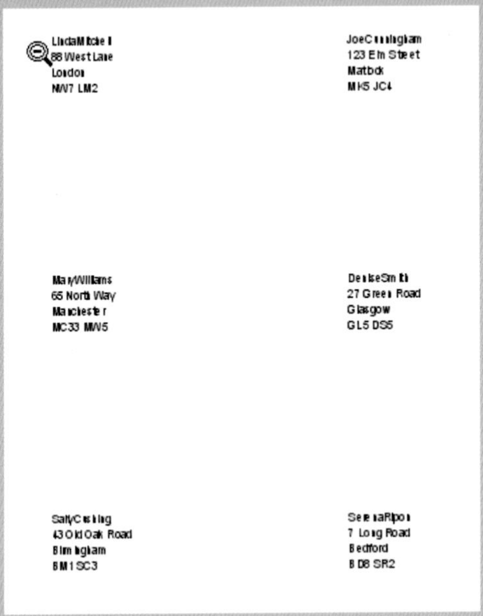

Figure 6.24: *The finished labels.*

> **! TIP**
>
> If you want to create a report that uses data from more than one table, base your report on a query.

Printing out reports

In order to meet the **Merit** and **Distinction** levels of the grading criteria, you need to be able to print out at least one report based on a database you have worked on. The activity below shows you how to do this.

Activity 7: Printing out data using reports...

In this activity you will:

* print out your report called **My Address Book**
* print out your report called **My Labels**.

▶ Double click the report called **My Address Book**.

▶ Select **Print** from the **File** menu to print the report.

▶ Click **OK** to close the **Print Window**.

▶ Double click the report called **My Labels**.

▶ Select **Print** from the **File** menu to print the report.

▶ Click **OK** to close the **Print Window**.

▶ Close Access.

Portfolio evidence

Based on the topic area that you have chosen in conjunction with your teacher or tutor, use the 'How to achieve' section at the beginning of this chapter to guide you in manipulating and maintaining a business database at the level towards which you are working.

The previous sections have given you some indication of how you could use database software correctly. You should think about:

* keeping your database up-to-date
* accurate data input
* using different report layouts to help present your information clearly
* using options within the software to work efficiently.

UNIT ⓵ 21

Creating Computer Graphics

In this unit you will cover the following...

➔ **AO1**   Research, collect and describe a range of existing graphics for use on web pages

➔ **AO2**   Write a production log detailing the origin of images, their source and how used, for the web page

➔ **AO3**   Create a navigation bar for the web page

➔ **AO4**   Design a set of navigation buttons

➔ **AO5**   Create an advertising banner

➔ **AO6**   Present work to a client for a specific purpose, using a suitable format for display

Introduction to Unit 21

This unit is one of the half units which you can combine with full units to gain full qualifications in this course. Creating computer graphics is a skill you may use in producing multimedia products, web design or desktop publishing and so the work you produce for this unit could be used to enhance the work you complete for other units.

This unit will focus on the use of Macromedia Fireworks software. Fireworks is a versatile graphics design package which incorporates many features that are suited to creating graphics for the web. You will work through a sample project which gives you the opportunity to practise working closely with the software.

It is recommended that you spend some time familiarising yourself with Fireworks and the various tools, applications and features it has to offer before you start work on the activities in AO2, 3, 4 and 5. The screenshot below shows the main elements of the software:

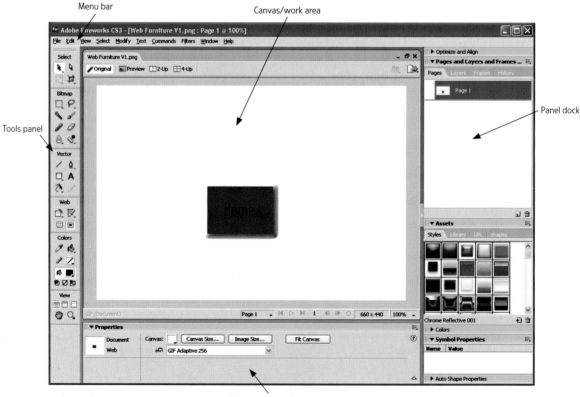

CHAPTER (7)

→ *Assessment Objective 1*

Researching, Collecting and Describing a Range of Existing Graphics

....

Overview:

Before you produce graphics and images, you need to carry out research into graphics and images that are used on the World Wide Web. This research will help you to decide on the content and quality of the graphics and images you create.

Assessment Objective 1 focuses upon the research you need to carry out to find out how a range of graphics and images are used on a variety of websites. You will then analyse the images and graphics so that you can identify purpose and impact, as well as identifying their positive and negative points. In this chapter, you will be shown how to decide on which images to analyse and how these may be collected. We will also discuss how you may describe each of the graphics and images you collect.

How this assessment objective will be assessed...

You will be assessed on:

- the amount of graphics and images you collect
- the quality and range of information you provide in your description of the graphics and images you collect
- the quality of the reasons you provide to back up the comments you make about the graphics and images you collect.

Skills to use...

- You will need to use imagination in your choice of graphics and images. Your discussion of the graphics and images you collect will need to be clearly presented with well thought-out supporting arguments that back up the points you make.

How to achieve...

Pass requirements

P1 You should collect and display examples of graphics from at least two different websites.

P2 You should describe the purpose of the graphics you have collected.

P3 Comment on the positive and negative aspects of the graphics you have collected.

Merit requirements

M1 You should collect and display examples of graphics from at least three different websites.

M2 You should describe the graphics you have collected. This description will include:

o the purpose of each graphic

o the suitability for purpose of each graphic

o details of the size of each graphic.

M3 Comment on the positive and negative aspects of the graphics you have collected, giving reasons for your decisions.

Distinction requirements

D1 You should collect and display examples of graphics from at least four different websites.

D2 You should describe the graphics you have collected. This description will include:

o the purpose of each graphic

o the suitability for purpose of each graphic

o details of the size of each graphic.

D3 Comment on the positive and negative aspects of the graphics you have collected, giving valid reasons for your decisions.

Graphics and images

Before we carry on, we need to sort out the terms we are going to use in this chapter. The subject specification for this unit uses the terms graphics/images whenever it talks about what you or I might call 'pictures'. The problem here is that 'pictures' is rather vague and is not really the technical term. However, it is probably not a good idea to use the term 'graphics/images' either. To avoid confusion, we will use the term **graphics** to mean anything that you may call a picture or an image.

Key terms

Computer graphics

Any form of picture that may be shown on a computer.

Researching graphics

Your work for this assessment objective will be based on existing web graphics which you will find and then present, with a commentary. The first part of this activity will be to research into graphics. To a large extent, your choice of graphic will depend on the project you complete. However, whatever the focus of your research, the graphics you collect will be more useful to you if you plan your research before you begin.

Your task will be to look at a range of websites and describe how different types of graphics are used on them. As we shall see, your description could be a written report, but it is better if your report combines screenshots or downloaded graphics. In fact your report could even be a presentation, rather than a written report. If you choose to do a presentation, you would still need to include written analysis of your findings.

There are several types of graphics you should describe. These are:

- logos
- graphical navigation bars
- advertising banners
- navigational buttons
- web icons.

Logos

These are basically graphics which are associated with organisations, such as businesses, charities or schools. A good logo is one which is readily associated with the organisation which they represent. You should be able to find a logo on just about any business or other official website.

Graphical navigation bars

A navigation bar is a block of hyperlinks that are grouped together. A graphical navigation bar is one which uses graphics as hyperlinks, so that the user can click on a graphic to go to another web page.

Figure 7.1: *A graphical navigation bar.*

Advertising banners

An advertising banner is an advertisement which usually spans the width of the web page. Most advertising banners will combine together graphics and text.

Navigational buttons

Navigational buttons are graphics which act as a hyperlink. When you choose your navigational button you need to make sure that it is a button, as basically any web page element can have a hyperlink added to it. For example, you may find a large graphic which has a hyperlink attached to it. This would probably not count as a navigational button. As a basic rule of thumb, a navigational button should look like a button.

Web icons

An icon is a small graphic which has a very clear meaning. The small pictures at the top of any piece of software are icons and their purpose should be very clear. A web icon is specifically designed to appear on the World Wide Web.

Planning

There are many methods you could use to plan your research. However, one method you could use to start things off would be to mind map, based on the theme of your main project or a research task you have been given. Once you have completed your mind map, you should then have enough ideas to begin your research. Alternatively, you might be given a list of websites by your school on which you can base your research. Your research into the use of graphics on websites can be limited to how the different types of graphics are used on the first page of any website.

Activity 1: Researching graphics...

In this activity you will:

● find graphics for a specific purpose.

You have been asked to provide graphics of an area for use by an estate agent's office. Before you begin the task of creating these, you have been asked to provide eight graphics as examples of the sort of graphics you would like to create. The graphics you choose at this stage need not be of your local area.

▶ Using any planning method you wish, decide on the graphics you will find.

▶ Using any source you wish, find eight suitable graphics. Make a note of where these have been found. We will be looking at how to use the graphics you discover below. You may want to jump ahead and check the next section if you want to complete this task in one go.

Acquiring graphics

Once you have found the graphics you will use, you need to display them. The choice of how you display the graphics is up to you but some of the methods are described below. However, there are two methods of collection which we need to discuss before we move on:

● copy and paste
● saving graphics for later use.

If you need to display the web page as a whole, the best method is to create a screenshot (see page 148).

Copy and paste

This is the simplest method of acquiring a graphic. For this method, you simply right click on the graphic and the **context menu** will appear.

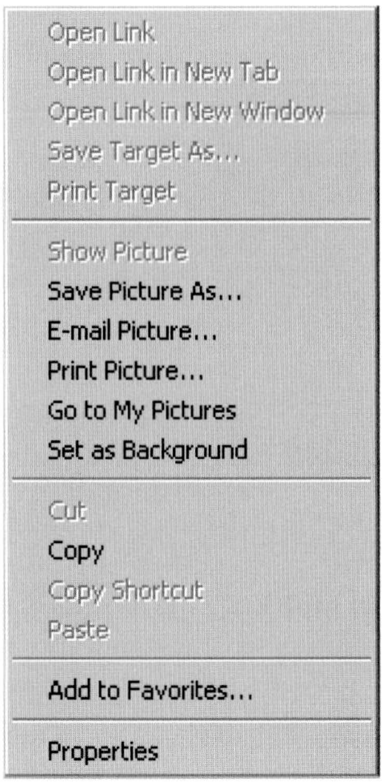

Open Link
Open Link in New Tab
Open Link in New Window
Save Target As...
Print Target

Show Picture
Save Picture As...
E-mail Picture...
Print Picture...
Go to My Pictures
Set as Background

Cut
Copy
Copy Shortcut
Paste

Add to Favorites...

Properties

Figure 7.2: *The graphic context menu.*

From this menu, you would choose the **copy** option. This will then create a copy of the image you selected and place it in the **clipboard** or **notepad** of your computer. This copy is then available for you to **paste** the graphic into your chosen target software.

Key terms

Context menu

Many different menus are available when you click the right hand mouse button. Because the menu which appears depends on what you click on, these are called context menus.

Clipboard

This is a temporary storage area on your computer – any materials you copy as part of the copy and paste process are placed in it. This area may also be called the notepad.

Saving graphics for later use

This option is also available from the graphic context menu. The **save** option allows you to save a copy of any graphic on which you right click, to your hard drive. This allows you to add a copy of the graphic to any document you choose.

Creating screenshots

Screenshots are created by pressing the **Print Screen** button. This is sometimes shown on the keyboard as Print Screen or is shortened to **Prt Scr** or **PrtSc**. When you click on this button, a graphic of what is shown on the computer screen is saved to the clipboard for you to use later. This may be pasted into a word processing or other document.

Activity 2: Acquiring graphics...

In this activity you will:

● save the graphics you found in Activity 1.

▶ Create a directory called **unit 21** in your work area.

▶ Use the graphic context menu to **save** the graphics you found in Activity 1 into the unit 21 directory you have just created.

Displaying graphics

There are many ways you can display the graphics you collect. Some of these are listed below.

● Create a presentation using presentation software such as *Microsoft PowerPoint*.
● Create a formal written report using word processing software.
● Create a brochure using desktop publishing software.
● Create your own website which includes the images. If you completed this option and published your website on the Internet, you would need to be aware of copyright issues.

Describing graphics

The final task for Assessment Objective 1 is to describe the graphics you have collected. If you are aiming for a **Pass**, your description should include:

● the purpose of the graphic
● the positive and negative aspects of the graphic.

If you are aiming for a **Merit**, your description should include:

● the purpose of the graphic
● the suitability of the graphic for the purpose
● the size of the graphic
● the positive and negative aspects of the graphic, including reasons for your decision.

If you are aiming for a **Distinction**, your description should include:

● the purpose of the graphic
● the suitability of the graphic for the purpose
● the impact of the graphic
● the size of the graphic
● the positive and negative aspects of the graphic, including **valid** reasons for your decision.

Describing the purpose of graphics

Graphics used on web pages or magazines are not chosen at random. They are the result of a selection process that whittles graphics down from a large choice to a final few, which all suit the web page, article or advert on which they are to be used. You need to develop the ability to choose the most suitable graphic for your work. Describing the purpose of graphics chosen and used by other people is an important stage in developing this skill.

Graphics can be used for many different purposes including to:

- make a point
- clarify a point or explanation
- give an example
- shock
- entertain
- attract attention.

Graphics may also be used because of the role they play on the page. For example, they may be used to break up text on a page so that it looks more interesting. However, while this may be one purpose of the graphic, the choice of which graphic to use will be based on the same criteria as any other graphic used.

When you need to decide on the purpose of your graphic, try to get a feel for the context in which the graphic was used. This may be achieved by reading the text or looking at other images used in the same context.

Target audience

Part of your basic description of your graphic needs to include a description of the **target audience**. You will probably have come across this term in other books in this series. However, if you have not, this is a quick explanation.

Target audience is a very important concept: it is the group of people at whom a product is aimed. For a general product, such as a type of food eaten by a wide range of people, there would be a very large target audience. An example of such a product could be burgers sold in a chain of restaurants. Many different types of people will eat food like this and so the advertising and publicity for this product need to be quite general. However, for other products, such as specialist books, there will be a very narrow target audience, as only people who are interested in the subject matter for the book would buy it. An example of this could be books of locomotive numbers published for train spotters. Any train spotters reading this book will now be protesting that this is not a narrow interest and there are thousands of people who share the hobby. However, even the keenest train spotter will accept that there are more people who eat burgers than spot trains and so will accept that the book itself, as well as any advertising, must appeal to that relatively narrow target audience.

Key terms

Target audience

The group of people to which a graphic is intended to appeal.

The suitability of the graphic used

We have already explained that the choice of which graphic to use on a page will be the result of a long selection process. However, mistakes can be made during this process.

Alternatively, the graphics you choose may be the most suitable ever chosen. Your task is to make a decision about how well the graphics you choose fit their purpose. Obviously, this will depend on how well you have identified the purpose. If the purpose you described is not quite the same as the purpose which was originally identified, you may have a problem. However, it is probably better to ignore this possibility and assume that you have correctly identified the purpose.

Therefore, the suitability of the graphic is how well it does the task for which it was chosen. For example, if you decide that a graphic has been included to inform, you must then decide whether the graphic informs. If it does, then you can comment that the graphic you have chosen is suitable for the purpose. Alternatively, if you decide that the graphic does not inform, then clearly the graphic is not suitable for purpose.

There are a number of areas you could analyse to help you make your decision about how suitable the graphic is. You could consider:

- The content of the graphic
  - Is there anything in the graphic that does not suit the product?
  - Is there anything in the graphic that does not suit the target audience?
- The quality of the graphic
  - Is the graphic pixelated?
  - Is the graphic the correct size?
  - Do the colours of the graphic suit the purpose? Would the graphic be more suitable if it was in black and white?

The impact of graphics

One last area to describe is the impact of a graphic. Some graphics have a far greater impact than others, especially when those graphics have been chosen to either show or induce emotion in the audience. Graphics chosen to support a charity appeal are a good example of graphics that are intended to induce a reaction from the audience. Similarly, newspaper articles, especially from war zones or from disasters, are generally chosen to maximise the effect they have on the audience.

Your task for this aspect of your description of graphics is to try to gauge what effect a graphic could have. This might be the intended effect on the target audience, or it might be an unintentional effect on an entirely different audience.

The size of the graphic

This part of your description deals with the physical size of the graphic on the page, in which case you may talk about the percentage of the page which the graphic covers, as well as the actual size of the graphic file.

If you have used other software titles within the Macromedia suite, such as Flash, you will not be surprised to find that Fireworks has a **properties** panel at the bottom of the screen. As with other titles in the Macromedia suite, the properties panel shows a good deal of information about the graphic on which you are working.

Figure 7.3: The properties panel.

By far the simplest way of finding the file size of a graphic is to hover the mouse over the file icon in Windows Explorer. After a short period of time, the file size of the graphic will appear.

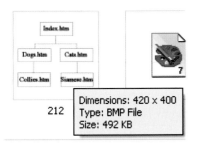

Figure 7.4: *Using Windows Explorer to display the file size.*

Describing the positive and negative aspects of the graphic

As well as the actual image, you may want to describe the overall quality of a graphic. Clearly, if the website or other source from which you have chosen the graphic wants to present a professional image, it is probably better not to have poor quality graphics.

Poor quality graphics would include those that are pixellated or where the graphic is blurred or has been badly edited. You should include comments on any of these aspects if you consider them necessary. Alternatively, if the graphics you choose have been well edited, or are very clear with no **pixellation**, these are all areas where you could make positive comments.

Other areas on which you could comment might include the colours in the graphic or the actual subject matter of the graphic. Your judgement of these factors would depend on the purpose of each graphic.

Key terms

Pixel

A pixel is the single dot of a graphic.

Pixellation

This is the effect when a picture is zoomed in on. As you zoom in on the picture, so the dots become more apparent. A pixellated graphic is one which has been resized so that the individual dots of colour are very obvious.

Activity 3: Presenting and describing graphics...

In this activity you will:

- present and describe the graphics you found and saved in Activities 1 and 2.

▶ Using any method you choose, present and describe the graphics you found in Activity 1.

CHAPTER (8)

→ *Assessment Objective 2*

Planning a Range of Graphic Images for a Client's Website

· ·

Overview:

This chapter leads on from the research you did in Chapter 7. Here, you will learn how to produce sketch plans for three web elements. The quality of your plans, including the detail, will determine the grade you achieve for this assessment objective.

How this assessment objective will be assessed...

You will be assessed on:

- the amount of detail included in the plans you produce
- the amount of supporting detail for each of the plans you produce. This should include:
  - details of the target audience
  - the purpose of each graphic you plan to create
- the quality and relevance of the house style you identify, as well as the extent to which you apply it to your plans
- the extent to which the size of each graphic is taken into consideration.

Skills to use...

- Your designs will need to show accuracy and imagination.
- You will need to create a suitable house style and use it in the design of your web elements.

How to achieve...

Pass requirements

P1 You will produce basic sketch diagrams for three different types of graphic.

P2 You will provide some details about your target audience and purpose.

Merit requirements

M1 You will produce detailed sketch diagrams for three different types of graphic.

M2 You will provide details about your target audience and purpose.

M3 You will identify and use a house style for your graphics.

M4 You will show some consideration of the file size of the graphic.

Distinction requirements

D1 You will produce comprehensive details for the three different types of graphic you plan to create, accompanied by detailed sketch diagrams.

D2 You will provide details about your target audience and purpose.

D3 You will identify and use a house style for your graphics.

D4 You will show consideration of the file size of the graphic.

Sketch plans

Throughout this chapter, you will be asked to create sketch plans or diagrams. These are exactly what they sound like. You do not need to use software for these plans – a pen and paper will do. The difference between each of the grade bands lies in the detail you include with your plans. You will find that the rest of this chapter deals with the detail you need to include, rather than how to draw lovely pictures. This is because lovely pictures will not get you good grades, but good planning and lots of relevant detail will!

Supporting details

We discussed three of the main areas which you need to include in your plans in the previous chapter. As a quick reminder, these were:

- target audience
- purpose/message
- size.

You will already have covered these elements in your review of the use of graphics in Chapter 7. However, there is one further element you need to include in your planning. This is **House style**.

House style

House style refers to the use of standard elements, such as colours or font style or size, to create a common standard or 'look' for your graphics. If you are successful, anyone who is familiar with the graphics you create should be able to recognise any other graphic that you have designed, using the same house style, as being your work. Therefore, the house style is the subtle (and not so subtle) clues that allow a reader to recognise the work of one person or group of people.

The first stage of creating a house style is to decide on how elements of your graphics will look. At this stage, you will be making decisions about the colours, quality, size and type of graphic you will be creating. You may also go on to decide on the quality of printing or of paper you use, if the graphics you produce are to be printed off. However, we are concerned with web elements in Assessment Objective 2, so this is not strictly relevant to this discussion. Once you have made these decisions, they will only be a house style if you use them consistently – so make sure that you do.

The decisions you make may be influenced by many factors. The two most important factors will be the target audience and the needs of the brief. If you are aiming at a younger target audience, but wish to establish an academic atmosphere, you will be likely to choose a different house style for graphics to be used on a project aimed at young people, but for a more light-hearted project.

The graphics below show two graphical elements which have been created using a house style. This project is one to create buttons for a website for young children. The developers of the website are hoping that it will become an internationally used resource and so have asked that any graphics used are internationally recognisable.

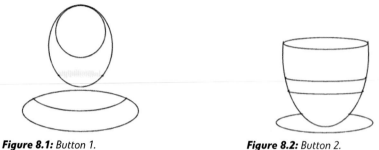

Figure 8.1: *Button 1.*   **Figure 8.2:** *Button 2.*

It should be clear that these buttons have both been created using the same house style. The first button is to open a web page about rings and the second is to open a web page about glasses. Both buttons have the same feel, colour scheme and, when on the same page, will be of the same size.

Activity 1: Create a house style

In this activity you will:

● design a number of house styles to use on graphics for different purposes.

The company for which you work has been asked to suggest house styles for use on graphics for the following projects. For each project, think of the needs of the target audience and of the brief. Use your decisions to suggest how different design considerations may be combined together to create a suitable house style. You should create two styles for each project.

Project 1: The 'Open House' young mums ICT access project

A locally funded project, which has been set up to allow young mothers to develop their ICT skills, wants to create a website. The website will need a logo, an advertising banner and a graphical navigation bar.

Project 2: A website for a Member of Parliament

You have been approached by Paul Welsh, a prospective independent Member of Parliament. He wishes to improve the look of his website. At present, the website appears dull and unappealing to anyone but the most committed politician. You have been asked to design a logo, advertising banner and buttons for use on the new website.

Designs which are fit for purpose, suit the target audience and fit the medium

Now that you have an understanding of how web furniture (the elements which are placed on a website to make them look more attractive) is designed, you need to bring these skills together to design some web elements. When you do so, you need to ensure that your designs are for elements which are fit for purpose, suit the needs of the target audience and fit the medium. These three concepts have been dealt with elsewhere but a little more clarification would be helpful.

'Fit for purpose' is an easy concept to understand and apply. If a graphic or any other design or device does what it is meant to do, it is fit for purpose. A pair of wellies that leak when you stand in a puddle are not fit for purpose, as their purpose is to keep people's feet dry when they stand in puddles. The 'target audience' is who the graphic or other design or product is aimed at. A range of wellies which only come in children's sizes are not suitable for adults – it is unlikely that many adults will be able to fit them on their feet.

Finally, 'fit for the medium' means that the graphic is suitable for use on the Web.

Activity 2: Designing graphics...

In this activity you will:

- take account of target audience, purpose, size and house style to design graphics.

The company for which you work has been asked to create an advertising banner and navigation buttons to use on a website for a vet's surgery called Pets love Vets. The developers of the website have already developed a house style for the website and this is explained below. You have been asked to create some designs for sample graphics which will meet the needs of the client, suit the target audience and fit the house style. You decide to design an **advertising banner,** a **home button** and a **navigation bar**.

The house style is for a simple presentation. Any graphics are to be simple black and white line drawings. The impression which the developers wish to give is that the graphics have been produced by a young person who is good at art, rather than a professional graphics artist. Any text on the website should be in a simple but bold font and should be in line with the developers' aim for black and white on the website.

The advertising banner needs to have the name of the vet's surgery. The developers have asked that there are also photographs of pets included as a background for the advertising banner. These may be laid out as blocks of photographs, or a few photographs may be merged together to create a montage of graphics. The graphics you eventually choose to create the finished product may be created by you or found elsewhere.

Produce the designs for the sample advertising banner, home button and navigation bar. Your sketches must include details of the house style to be used, the target audience of the website (and therefore the web furniture), and the size of the graphics and elements you intend to use.

⊕TIP

Remember that when you come to design your graphics, you must create at least three separate web elements. Your designs may include text as well as graphics and must be fit for purpose, be suitable for use on the Web and suit the target audience. To achieve a Distinction, your sketch diagrams must be detailed and give comprehensive details of what is being planned. 'Comprehensive details' basically means that your plans could be passed onto someone else; they could then create them almost as you would have done if you had created the finished product yourself.

CHAPTER (9)

⊕ *Assessment Objective 3*
Creating a Navigation Bar

. . . .

Overview:

A navigation bar is an excellent piece of web furniture which can give a web-site a really consistent feel. At the most basic level, a navigation bar (or menu bar, but we will use the term **navigation** bar) is a group of buttons which all look very much the same. This group of buttons then appears on every page. Obviously, by appearing on every page, a good navigation bar will go a long way towards establishing a consistent feel on the website.

More complex navigation bars add extra elements, such as drop-down menus. We will create one simple navigation bar. We will then go on to create a naviga-tion bar with more complex features.

The navigation bar you create need not include a huge number of pages. However, it must include as many as you need to give the person marking your work a clear indication of what you can do. As with any other course of this nature, the choice of which evidence to provide is yours to make. Your target is to achieve as good a grade as possible, so make sure you provide enough evidence for you to be given it.

Finally, you must show good use of your design skills. Navigation bars can be a really eye-catching part of a web page, but only if they are well designed. Your navigation bar needs to make good use of colour and will benefit from thoughtful use of contrasting colours, so that users are better able to follow any links.

How this assessment objective will be assessed...

You will be assessed on the following aspects of your website:

- the type and range of facilities you use in your navigation bar
- the colours you choose to create an 'easy to use' navigation bar
- the extent to which your navigation bar is fit for purpose
- the extent to which your navigation bar suits the needs of the target audience.

Skills to use...

- You will be expected to show good use of the design skills you developed for Assess-ment Objective 2 in Chapter 8. Your navigation bar should be consistent, with the use of standard and meaningful buttons or images which use colour to improve the ease with which users can access web pages.
- You need to show a good understanding of how colours combine and contrast.

How to achieve...

Pass requirements

P1 You will produce a basic navigation/menu bar that uses some colour.

P2 Your navigation/menu bar will be suitable for purpose.

P3 Your navigation/menu bar will be based on a table.

Merit requirements

M1 You will produce a navigation/menu bar that makes good use of colour.

M2 Your navigation/menu bar will be suitable for purpose and audience.

M3 Your navigation/menu bar will make use of graphic and text which will be well combined.

Distinction requirements

D1 You will produce an effective navigation/menu bar that makes good use of colour.

D2 Your navigation/menu bar will be fit for purpose and audience.

D3 Your navigation/menu bar will make use of drop-down boxes or expanding/collapsing menus.

Things to consider

A lot of the grading for Unit 21 is based on the extent to which your navigation bar is fit for purpose and meets the needs of the target audience. We discussed these two concepts in Chapter 7 (Assessment Objective 1) and you should be happy to assess these aspects of other people's work. Now is the time for you to apply this understanding to your own work. Remember to have a very clear idea about what you are trying to create before you put your fingers anywhere near your keyboard. The planning you do, which was the subject of Chapter 8 (Assessment Objective 2), must make clear reference to the needs of the target audience, as well as the purpose of the piece of web furniture you are creating.

Colour contrast

It is worth spending a little time talking about contrasting colours before we continue. You need to be aware that if you use contrasting colours, your work will be easier to use. However, if you do not have sufficient contrast between your background colours and the colours you use for elements such as text, many users will find the elements you create difficult to use. In fact, the use of colours which do not contrast may be considered sufficient evidence to show that your work was not fit for purpose.

There are three things you should avoid:

- Do not use dark coloured text on dark backgrounds, such as blue on green.
- Do not use light coloured text on light backgrounds, such as yellow on white.
- Do not use multi-coloured images as backgrounds.

Creating the navigation bar

There are two ways in which you could create a navigation bar. The first would be to create a table layout and add graphics and/or text into each cell of the table. Each graphic or piece of text would then act as a hyperlink.

Alternatively, you could create a series of drop-down menus which allow the user access to a themed group of hyperlinks. We will begin by creating a table-based navigation bar.

Naming elements

As you work through this and other chapters in this unit, you will be asked to create and name objects. It is better that you choose meaningful names for any objects you create. By meaningful names, we mean names which mean something and are linked to the object or the task the object will do. 'My first button' might mean something to you but it is not the best name. 'Standard navigation button v1' may not seem so exciting, but it is far more meaningful and will make your work easier as you create more objects.

The assignment for this unit

The work you produce for this unit will be based on a commission from two comedians, Les Gets and Des Trunks. Les and Des were huge stars in the 1970s and filled concert halls throughout the UK, although they never ever played abroad. Their style was very much based on what they had learned playing the clubs in the north of England. At one stage, they had a television series called 'Up North with Les and Des', which allowed them to show their unique brand of humour to a wider audience.

Unfortunately, tastes change and Les and Des did not survive the wave of alterative comedy which grew up at the end of the 1970s. However, they feel the time is right for a comeback. They have booked a series of venues and now want a website to help publicise their forthcoming tour. You will be producing a range of elements for this website. We will be using Fireworks, which is part of the Macromedia suite of software titles, to produce these elements.

Using the ruler and gridlines

We need to discuss the use of two tools before we go on. There is going to be a lot of close up work in this unit. The work you produce must be well laid out and look professional. The best way to do this is to use the ruler and to show gridlines.

Both **rulers** and **gridlines** are part of the **view** sub-menu. When you make rulers visible, a ruler appears along the top of the page and along the side. As you move the cursor, so your position on the x-axis (the horizontal) is shown on the ruler along the top of the page and the position on the y-axis (the vertical) is shown on the ruler along the side of the page. These side and top rulers help you to position your work.

Gridlines are part of the **Grid** sub-menu off the **view** sub-menu. If you choose **Show Grid**, a grid is shown. This will also help you to organise the layout of your work.

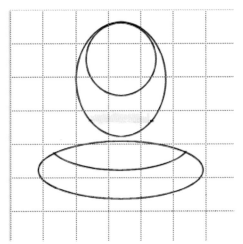

Figure 9.1: *The use of grids helps you to organise your work.*

Creating a table-based navigation bar

The table-based navigation bar is based on groups of buttons. Assessment Objective 4 deals specifically with buttons and how these may be created. In this exercise we will cover a few of the basics of creating grouped buttons. We will expand on this understanding in Chapter 10.

Activity 1: Creating a navigation bar and adding a button...

In this activity you will:

- create a navigation bar
- create a button within the navigation bar.

▶ Choose **File...New** to create a new file. This file needs to be 500 pixels wide and 75 pixels high. This file will be the navigation bar.

▶ Now use the rectangle tool to create a rectangle which is 125 pixels wide and 75 pixels high. You should try to draw this freehand but, if you are not totally accurate, you can make any necessary changes to the rectangle by changing the settings for the rectangle in the **Properties Inspector**.

▼ Properties		
Rectangle	Solid	
	Edge: Anti-Alias ▼ 0	
W: 125 X: 71	Texture: Grain ▼ 0 ▼	
H: 75 Y: 180	☐ Transparent	

Figure 9.2: *The rectangle shape.*

▶ Now fill the rectangle you have created with a solid colour fill. This is done by choosing the **Paint Bucket** tool. Hit **escape** on the keyboard and then choose the **Select** tool.

▶ With the rectangle selected, look to the right of the **Properties Inspector panel**. There will be an area labelled **Filters**. Click on the **+** sign to bring up the list of available effects. Choose **Bevel and Emboss...Inner Bevel**.

You should now see that your rectangle looks far more like a button.

Figure 9.3: *The button-shaped object you have just created.*

Adding the interactivity – making the button 'move'

Well done! You now have a button-shaped object within a navigation bar. However, just because it looks like a button, this does not mean it behaves like a button. With most buttons, when you click them, something happens. We will now add the 'something happens' to the button you have just created.

Activity 2: Adding interactivity...

In this activity you will:

● add an event to your button.

▶ You need to convert your rectangle to a symbol. Choose **Modify...Symbol...Convert to Symbol** (F8 is the shortcut key). Give the new symbol a suitable name and select the **Button** radio button.

▶ You should now see that your button is shrouded in green mist and has an arrow at the bottom right. The arrow shows that your button has now been added to the list of symbols in your library. This means that you can use the button again later.

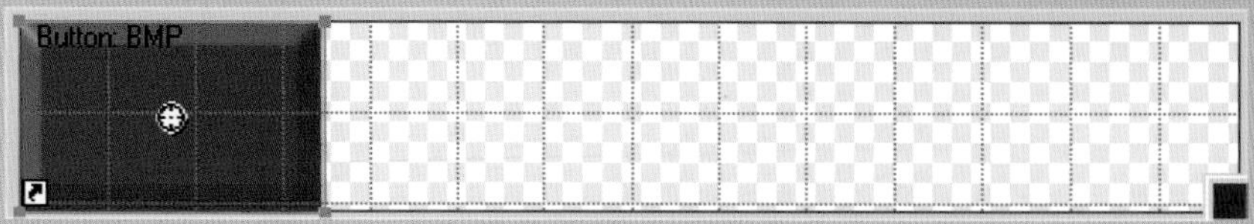

Button: BMP

Figure 9.4: *The button with added green mist.*

You are now ready to set the behaviour of the button. The behaviour includes what it does.

▶ Choose the **Select** tool and double click the button. The **Button Editor** will now open.

▶ Click on the **Active Area** tab. You will see that the graphic has now been broken into **Slices**. These **Slices** are shown by the red lines which are covering the graphic. The active area, which is the bit where the user will be clicking, is the green area.

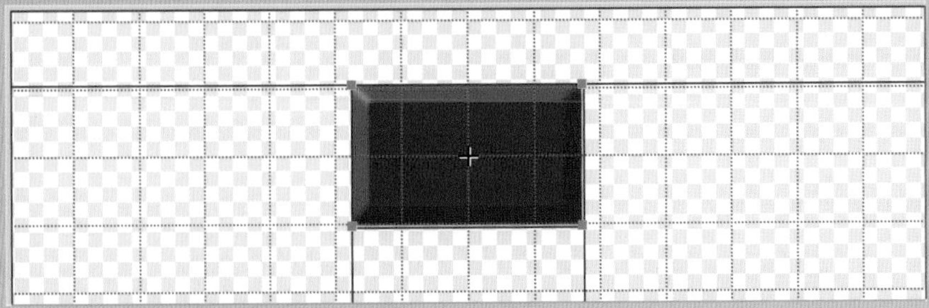

Figure 9.5: *The active area of the graphic.*

The other four tabs allow us to create a different look for our button depending on whether the button is up, has a mouse over it, down (pushed in) or has a mouse over it while down. We have created the **Up** state already and so we will only be making changes for the **Down** state.

▶ Choose the **Over tab**. Click on **Copy Up Graphic**. Click on **Down** and click on **Copy Over Graphic**. You should now have a copy of the **Up** graphic (the bevelled rectangle) displayed on your screen.

▶ Select the rectangle and then double click the **Inner Bevel** effect in the list of effects shown on the **Inspection Panel**. Choose **Inverted** from the button preset drop-down menu.

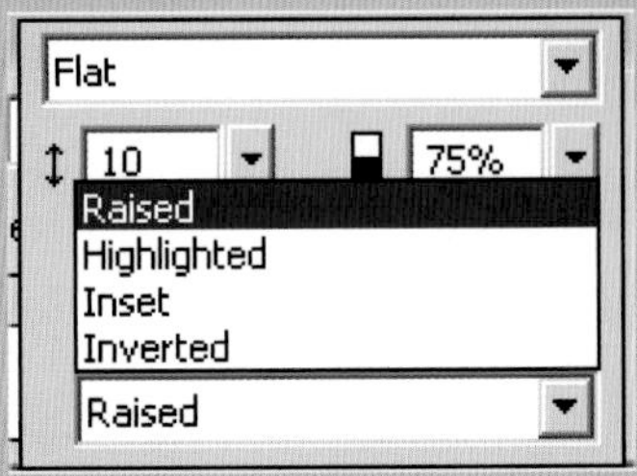

Figure 9.6: *The button preset menu.*

▶ Choose the **Over while Down** tab and click on the **Copy Down Graphic** button. Close the **Button Editor**. You can now test your button by selecting the **Preview** and clicking on the button.

Add text to the button

We've got a great looking button, but no text! We now need to add some text to the button so that users know what it is for.

Activity 3: Adding text to a button...

In this activity you will:

- add text to your button
- work with layers.

▶ Select your button and choose **Modify...Symbol...Convert to Symbol**. Name your symbol **Text and Image button** and select the **Button** radio button.

It is better if any text you add to your button is kept separate to the actual button itself. This makes it easier to edit later. To keep the text separate, we will be creating a separate layer which will hold the text.

▶ If the **Library panel** is not open, open it now (choose **Window...Library**). You will notice a small icon beside the name of the text and image button. This icon opens the **Button Editor**. Make sure that you are working with the **Text and Image button** and then click on this icon.

▶ Open the **Layers** panel. The button layer is in **Layer 1**. If you wish to make your work easier, you should double click on this layer and give the layer a meaningful name.

▶ Create a new layer by clicking on the **New/Duplicate Layer** button. You should also rename this layer. Select the new layer. You should be in the **Up** view.

▶ Choose the **Text** tool. Click on the 'Button that was a rectangle' which you have just created. Choose a font and font colour which suits your choice of background colour for the button (remember the section on contrast, above). A font size of about 20 to 25 should suit your needs.

▶ Add the text **Open** to your button. Use the **Select** tool to reposition your text if it is not quite correct.

You can add further effects to your text should you wish, but this is enough for our example.

▶ With the text selected, choose **Edit...Copy**. This will copy the text and not the whole of the button. Paste (**Edit...Paste**) the text onto the **Over** and **Down** button states. Every time you add the text, a new layer should be added to each button state.

▶ Close the button editor.

> **(!)TIP**
>
> In the last exercise, we copied and pasted rather than use the Copy from Up type button. This is because we only wanted to copy the text, as the buttons already existed.

Creating the navigation bar

We have now created our standard button. We will now use this standard button to create the navigation bar.

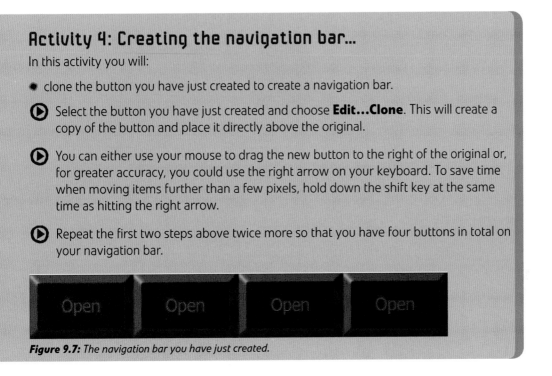

Activity 4: Creating the navigation bar...

In this activity you will:

- clone the button you have just created to create a navigation bar.

▶ Select the button you have just created and choose **Edit...Clone**. This will create a copy of the button and place it directly above the original.

▶ You can either use your mouse to drag the new button to the right of the original or, for greater accuracy, you could use the right arrow on your keyboard. To save time when moving items further than a few pixels, hold down the shift key at the same time as hitting the right arrow.

▶ Repeat the first two steps above twice more so that you have four buttons in total on your navigation bar.

Figure 9.7: *The navigation bar you have just created.*

Making the buttons unique

You now have a navigation bar with four identical buttons. We need to amend the text so that it is clear what each button does. We then need to add the URL (the website address) for each button.

We will begin by using the **Properties Inspector** panel to change the text on each button.

Creating unique text and adding the URL

You will now be adding URLs to your buttons. We will not be giving you URLs to which your buttons must link. For this practice assignment, choose four URLs which you will use.

Activity 5: Adding text and a URL to each button...

In this activity you will:

- add text to each button
- add a unique URL to each button.

▶ Select the left most button.

▶ In the **Properties Inspector**, you will see the current text for the button (**Open**) in the text field.

▶ Change this text to suit the URL you are going to assign to it (you could choose the name of the website to which you are linking or some other, descriptive, name).

▶ In the **Link** field, type in the full URL of the website to which you wish to link. This must start with http://www. If, for example, you were going to link to the Heinemann website, you would need to add: http://www.heinemann.com

▶ Repeat steps 1 to 4 for each of the other buttons to complete your navigation bar.

Congratulations! You have now created a navigation bar!

More complex navigation bars

If you are targeting a **Distinction** grade, you must include either a drop-down menu or an expanding/collapsing menu. These are basically the same thing. Once you have created a button, it is quite an easy task to create a drop-down menu in Fireworks.

Adding a pop-up menu

'Pop-up menus' is the term which Fireworks uses for drop-down menus. A completed pop-up is shown in Figure 9.8. In this exercise, you will be creating a pop-up menu with links to five websites of your choice. You could choose to use the same URLs as you used in Activity 5.

Figure 9.8: *A completed pop-up menu.*

Activity 6: Creating a pop-up menu...

In this activity you will:

● create a pop-up menu with links to five websites.

▶ Choose **File…New** to create a new file. This file needs to be 150 pixels wide and 150 pixels high. This file will be the button which users click to activate the pop-up menu.

▶ Follow the steps in **Activities 1 and 2** on pages 153–155 to create a button.

▶ Choose **Modify…Pop-up Menu…Add Pop-up Menu**. This will bring up the **Pop-up Menu Editor**.

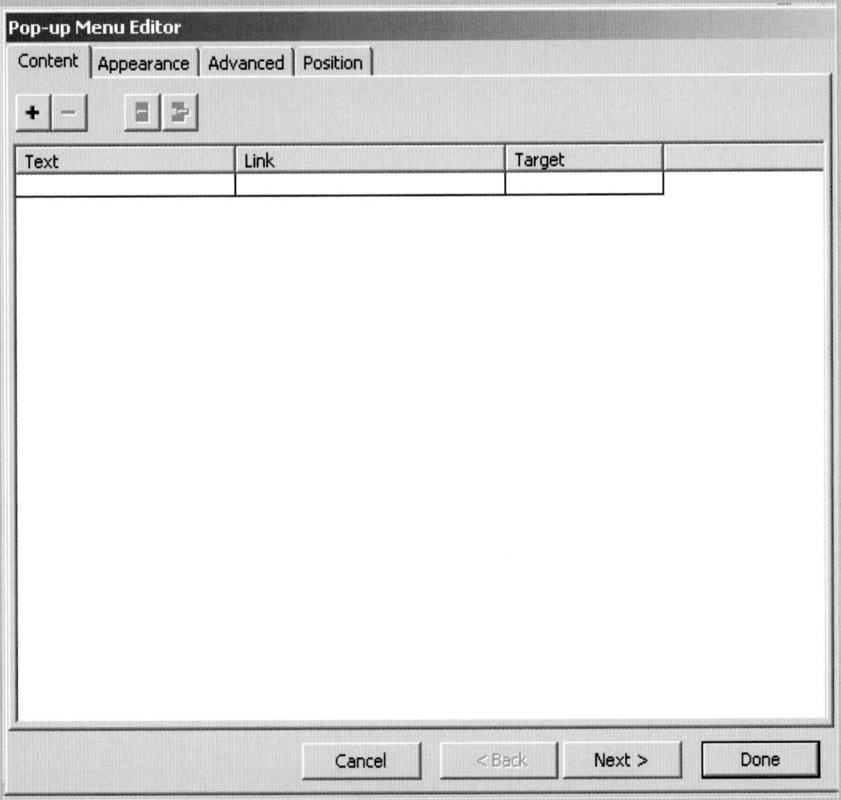

Pop-up Menu Editor

Content | Appearance | Advanced | Position

Text	Link	Target	

Cancel | < Back | Next > | Done

Figure 9.9: *The Pop-up Menu Editor.*

▶ Select the **Text** frame. Enter the text which will appear for your first menu item. This will be the text on which the user clicks to access web pages.

▶ Select the **Link** frame. Enter the URL for the website to which you are linking.

▶ You now need to set the target frame. This will be where the website you are going to link to the button opens.

▶ Double click on the **Target** frame. This will open up a drop down menu. Choose **_self**.

▶ Repeat steps 4–7 to create the four remaining links. Your completed **Pop-up Editor** should look something like the one shown below.

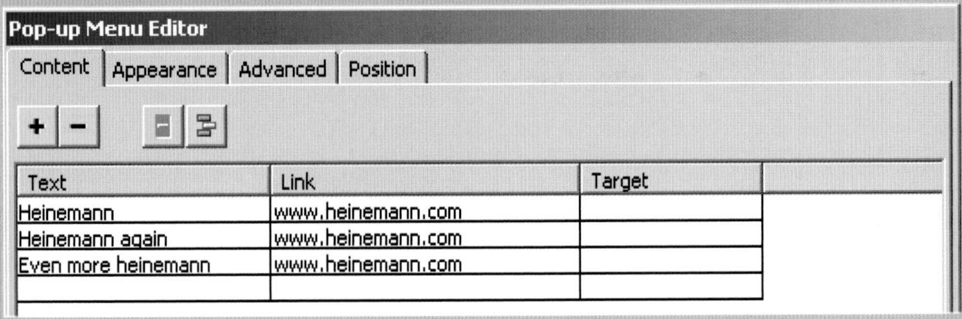

Pop-up Menu Editor

Content | Appearance | Advanced | Position

Text	Link	Target	
Heinemann	www.heinemann.com		
Heinemann again	www.heinemann.com		
Even more heinemann	www.heinemann.com		

Figure 9.10: *The completed Pop-up Menu Editor.*

⊙ The other options within the **Pop-up Menu** allow you to make changes to how the pop-up menu looks. The **Appearance** and **Advanced** tabs will both bring up a list of design choices. You can either access these by clicking on the **Next** button or by selecting the relevant tab.

⊙ The final option is where the pop-up menu appears once the button is clicked. The menu choices for this pop-up menu are accessed by clicking on the **Position** tab. The choices are clear.

Producing evidence

As well as presenting the electronic files themselves, or screenshots of the navigation bar you have created, the specifications for this unit require you to produce printouts which show enough detail to display the full capability of your system. Screenshots should show what you have created. For a basic navigation bar without a pop-up menu, you would need to show some evidence of the layout of the bar – a simple screenshot of the bar itself should be fine. You would also need to provide evidence that the buttons on the navigation bar do actually link to websites. A screenshot of the **Properties Inspector** panel with URLs shown would probably be sufficient evidence.

If you produce a pop-up menu, screenshots of the sub-menus on display would seem to be good evidence. You should also provide evidence of the URLs to which each text item links. A screen dump of the completed pop-up menu editor, as shown in Figure 9.10 would probably be sufficient evidence that you have created this element.

CHAPTER ⑩

→ *Assessment Objective 4*

Creating a Set of Navigation Buttons

. . . .

Overview:

In this chapter, you will be learning how to create interactive buttons which allow the user to move from one web page to another. The test of a graphical button is how much it actually looks like a real button, so we will look at how you can use the tools available within Fireworks to create a realistic button.

> In order to complete the activities in this chapter you will need access to a number of additional files. These files are contained in the Chapter 10 Resources zip file which can be downloaded from the OCR Nationals in ICT (Units 1 and 21) Student Resources page on the Payne-Gallway website: www.payne-gallway.co.uk.

- **Les and Des 1.jpg**
- **Les and Des 2.jpg**
- **Les and Des 3.jpg**

How this assessment objective will be assessed...

You will be assessed on the following aspects of your work:

- the amount of buttons you create (you must create a minimum of three)
- the extent to which your buttons are suitable for purpose
- the extent to which they suit the needs of the target audience.

Skills to use...

- You will need to have a good understanding of the tools available within the software to render objects to make them appear three dimensional. (It is worth noting that although three dimensional buttons may look better and be suitable for purpose and audience, there is no technical requirement for the buttons to appear three dimensional.) The tools and techniques explained in this chapter include many options, not all of which can be explained here. You are advised to work through the tasks included in this chapter with the materials provided, and to then repeat the tasks; you can either use the same resources or use graphics of your own, changing the settings and options taken as you do so. This will then give you a better understanding of the facilities on offer in the software and should improve the quality of your completed product.

How to achieve...

Pass requirements

P1 You will produce three buttons.

P2 Your buttons will either be based on ready-made templates or will be created by adapting graphics that already exist.

Merit requirements

M1 You will produce three buttons.

M2 Your buttons will be created from scratch or by customising ready-made templates.

M3 Your buttons will be suitable for purpose.

Distinction requirements

D1 You will produce three interactive buttons.

D2 Your buttons will be created from scratch or by customising ready-made templates.

D3 Your buttons will be suitable for purpose and audience.

Things to consider

In Chapter 8 (Assessment Objective 2), we discussed designing different web elements; we called these elements 'web furniture'. In Chapter 9, we looked at producing navigation bars by combining buttons. The design skills we covered in Chapter 8, and which you used in Chapter 9, will be as important in this chapter as they were in the last.

You will be producing at least three buttons. As you might expect, we will work through an example and then you will be asked to produce some buttons for practice. The buttons you produce will all carry on the theme of the last chapter, which was **The Les and Des website**.

When you produce the three buttons, you will need to consider three separate ideas. These are:

- suitability for purpose and audience
- interactivity
- the combination of graphics and text.

We have already dealt with **suitability for purpose and audience** in previous chapters, so we do not need to discuss these issues again here. However, we do need to consider the other two issues before we actually create the navigation buttons.

Interactivity

You will have come across the term 'interactive' before. For example, an interactive multi-media presentation is one with which the viewer can become physically involved and, by clicking on buttons, change the course of the presentation. In this context, interactivity is concerned with how well the user can work with the navigation button you create. To a large extent, this is a question of how effectively the user feels they are interacting. There are two basic concepts which help the user to feel that they are interacting. These are:

- How much does the button *look* like a button?
- How much does the button *act* like a button when used?

At this stage of the project, we are only making the 'furniture'. We do not need to include these buttons on a website and, therefore, we do not need to turn buttons into functioning hyperlinks. However, it is probably better if you do assign at least a sample URL to buttons, if only to show that you can.

How much does the button *look* like a button?

Try out Activity 1 below. We will use the understanding you gain from this exercise to 'move things on a little'.

Activity 1: Assessing buttons...

In this activity you will:

- consider what makes a graphic look like a button.

The two graphics below (Figures 10.1 and 10.2) have been created as two buttons to use on a website.

Individually

▶ For each button, list three good and three not-so-good features.

▶ Choose one good feature and one not-so-good feature for each button. For each feature you have chosen, write an explanation of why you feel the feature is either good or not so good.

In a pair

▶ Compare your good and not-so-good features of each button with a partner. It is probably better to deal with each button in turn. Discuss your explanations, and as a pair, try to come up with **four** features of a good button.

Figure 10.1: Button 1.

Figure 10.2: Button 2.

Now you should have a better idea of what makes a good button. Hopefully, you will have found features which are good about both buttons, or maybe you didn't...

How much does the button *act* like a button when used?

This is a little difficult to show in a book so the best thing is for you to complete another exercise.

Activity 2: What do buttons do?

In this activity you will:

● consider what a button does.

This activity is best done as a small group activity.

As a group, create a mind map of what a button does when pressed. To help you, you could think about a real button, maybe on a door bell or lift. Alternatively, you could think about other examples of buttons used on software.

Hopefully, the last two activities will have allowed your group to think about the features which make a graphic look like a button and behave like one. The more your graphics look and feel like real buttons, the better the feeling of interactivity people will have when they use your buttons.

The combination of graphics and text

The specifications for Assessment Objective 4 make it clear that the buttons you design could create text and graphics, or may be text or graphics on their own. The choice is yours and, as the grading for this assessment objective is based on how well your graphics suit the purpose and the audience, this choice needs to be based on who will be using the graphics and for what purpose. You could use templates which are available to create buttons, but it is far more fun to create a button from scratch. If you want to explore the templates you should do so once you have learnt to create your own buttons.

We will work through an example of a series of buttons which combine text and graphics. By doing so, you will learn enough skills so that the buttons you design could combine text and graphics or could be solely text or graphics based. For a Pass level, existing graphics could be adapted instead of creating them from scratch or with the use of a template.

The button – the design stage

Below is a design for a button to use on the Les and Des website.

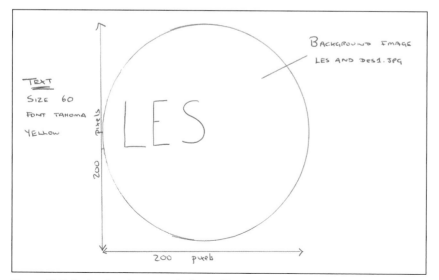

Figure 10.3: *Design for a button on the Les and Des website.*

We will now work through how to produce this button.

Creating the button-shaped graphic

We covered most of Activity 3 below in Chapter 9. However, there are a few extra skills included here which you may want to use. This activity also differs because you will be using an imported graphic as the button.

Activity 3: Creating the button-shaped graphic...

In this activity you will:

● create one button for the Les and Des website.

 Open Fireworks.

 Use the **File** menu to open the file **Les and Des 1.jpg**. You should have downloaded this graphic file at the beginning of this unit.

 Use the **Modify...Canvas...Image size** menu to resize this graphic so that it is 200 by 200 pixels. As the button you are about to create will be used on the Web, a resolution of 72 is fit for purpose. You will need to change the magnification to at least 200% so that you can work with this graphic.

We will now use the **text tool** to add text to the button.

 Select the **text tool**. This is in the **Vector** section of the tools panel. Use the vertical sliding bar to make the font size 60. Change the colour of the text so that it is Yellow. Finally, choose the Tahoma font from the drop-down font menu.

 Position the cursor on the left hand side of the graphic, about halfway down, and add the text: **Les**.

If the completed text does not sit properly on the page, use the **pointer tool** to select the text and reposition it, dragging and dropping to where you need it to go.

 You should now have two separate elements in your graphic. These two elements need to be combined into one. Use the **Modify...Merge down** menu to combine both elements of the graphic into one.

 You now have a merged graphic. However, it does not look much like a button.

We will start by selecting an area of the image which we will make into our button. We will use the **Oval Marquee** tool for this. Your software probably has the rectangular marquee by default. You can swap to the Oval Marquee tool by clicking on the small down arrow on the bottom right of the Marquee Tool button.

 Select the **Oval Marquee** tool. Set the **Edge** property to **anti-alias**.

 Use the tool to draw as near a perfect circle around the text as you can.

(►) We can now get rid of the bits outside of the circle, as we do not want them. Choose **Select...Select Inverse** to select the other area of the graphic (i.e. the part you have not selected by drawing a circle around it). If you now press **delete** on your keyboard, the parts you do not want disappear.

Figure 10.4: *The button-shaped graphic.*

> (!)**TIP**
>
> You need to know that most buttons in Fireworks have more than one tool attached to them. To swap between the tools, click on the small, downhill arrow on the bottom right of the button.

Adding the interactivity

Now you need to make your button *act* like a button. If you need some help with this topic, look back over the conclusions you came to about buttons in Activity 2. This activity is also an extension of Activity 2 included in Chapter 9.

Activity 4: Adding interactivity...

In this activity you will:

● learn how to make your button look like it has been pressed.

(►) Choose the **Select** tool and then click on the button-shaped graphic you have created. A blue rectangle should appear around it.

(►) Choose **Modify...Symbol...Convert to symbol**. From this menu, select **Button** and then click **OK**.

(►) The whole of your button-shaped graphic is now ready to become a button. It should look like it has become shrouded in green mist.

(►) With the **Select** tool still selected, double click on the button-shaped graphic to bring up the **Button Editor**. The button-shaped graphic has now appeared in the **Up** tab section. This is what your button will look like when the button is not being pushed. We need to make this look a bit more like a button.

(►) Click on the plus sign at the bottom right of the **Properties Inspector**. This will bring up the **Filters and Live effects** menu. Select **Eye Candy...Bevel boss**.

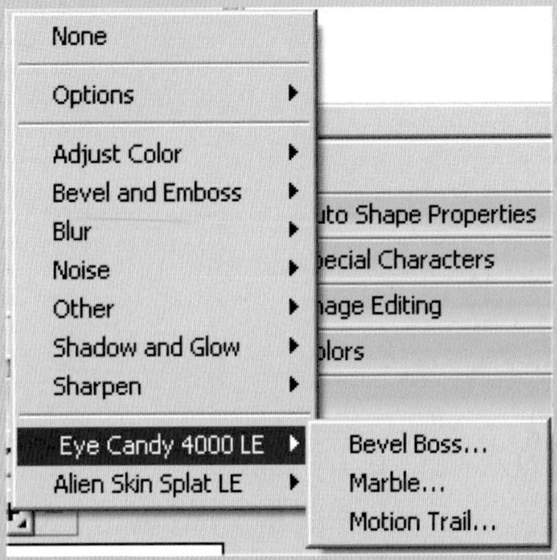

Figure 10.5: *The filters and live effects menu.*

▶ Copy the settings from the Bevel Boss Screen shot (Figure 10.6) and then click **OK**.

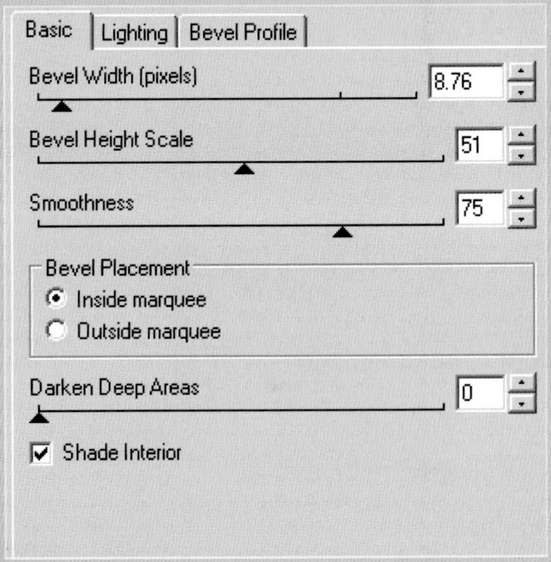

Figure 10.6: *Bevel Boss settings.*

▶ Select the **Over** tab and click the **Copy Up Graphic** button. We are not going to do anything to this state but we need to set what it looks like. The Up Graphic version of the button will now be pasted into the Over section.

We will now finish the transformation of our graphic so that when the button is clicked, it depresses, just like a normal, physical, button does.

▶ Select the **Down** tab. Click on the **Copy Over Graphic** button.

▶ Click on the plus at the bottom right by the Filters label and select **Bevel and Emboss...Inner bevel**. By default, you should be offered a Flat edge shape, with a width of 10. This should be enough to create the button effect, but feel free to play with the different settings. If you decide you do not like the setting you choose, you can change the settings for each filter later.

▶ Select the **Over While Down** tab and click on the **Copy Down Graphic**.

Add the default URL to your button

The final stage of creating a button is to add the default URL.

Activity 5: Adding navigation...

In this activity you will:

● learn how to add a default URL to a button.

▶ Select the **Active Area** tab. Your graphic will be sliced, with the main area that will be your button appearing in its own slice.

▶ Select the slice and the **Property Inspector** will now focus in on the slice which is the button slice. All property decisions you now make will only be applied to the slice.

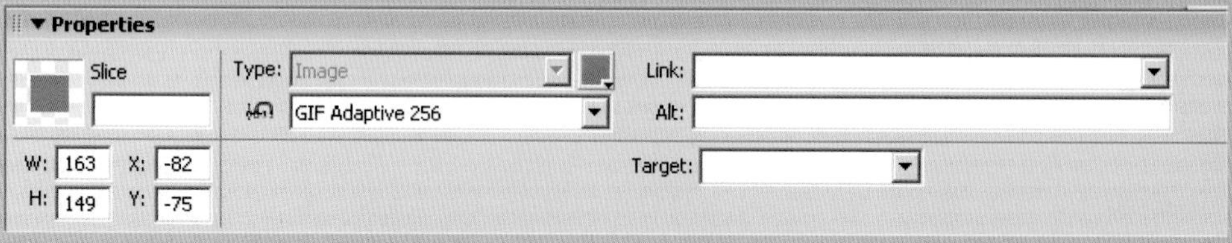

▼ Properties

Slice	Type: Image	Link:
GIF Adaptive 256	Alt:
W: 163 X: -82		Target:
H: 149 Y: -75		

Figure 10.7: The Slice Properties Inspector.

▶ Add a default URL into the **Link** box. At this stage, this might be your favourite search engine, or it might be your centre's website.

▶ Finally, type a description into the **Alt** box. This alternative text will be used if the viewer has turned off graphics in their web browser or while any page is loaded. The more descriptive the text, the better the viewer will know what is loading. The Alt text will also be visible when the mouse is moved over the graphic.

▶ Click **Done** to complete your button.

You have now created the first button. You might want to create others which change if the mouse is rolled over them. Your decision will depend on your plans, which should be based on the purpose of the button and the needs of the target audience.

Activity 6: More buttons...

In this activity you will:

● create the remaining two buttons.

The two remaining graphics for this chapter are **Les and Des 2.jpg** and **Les and Des 3.jpg**. (You should have downloaded these files at the start of this chapter.) Using the text **Des** for **Les and Des 2.jpg** and **Us!** for **Les and Des 3.jpg**, create two further buttons which are the same size as the first button.

CHAPTER ⑪
➔ *Assessment Objective 5*
Creating an Advertising Banner

Overview:

In this chapter, you will be working with text and graphics to create an advertising banner. You will be taken through the process of creating an animated banner which will also involve user interaction. Once you have mastered the techniques involved in creating this aspect of web furniture, you will be given further suggestions about how you may use these tools and techniques in your own work.

> In order to complete the activities in this chapter you will need access to an additional file. This file is contained in the Chapter 11 Resources zip file which can be downloaded from the OCR Nationals in ICT (Units 1 and 21) Student Resources page on the Payne-Gallway website: www.payne-gallway.co.uk.

● **Les and Des 4.jpg**

How this assessment objective will be assessed...

You will be assessed on the following aspects of your website:

● the amount of animation you include in your advertising banner
● the extent to which your advertising banner is fit for purpose
● the extent to which your advertising banner meets the needs of the target audience.

Skills to use...

● You will need to have a good understanding of how different layers operate within a graphic. It would also be helpful if you had an understanding of how frames are used to create animations.

How to achieve...

Pass requirements
P1 You will produce a static advertising banner.
P2 Your banner will combine text and graphics.

Merit requirements
M1 You will produce an advertising banner with some form of user interaction.
M2 Your banner will combine text and graphics.
M3 Your banner will be fit for purpose.

What is an advertising banner?

You might have completed units on desktop publishing where you learned what a banner headline is. If you have not, then basically, a banner headline is the feature at the top of a newspaper page which screams the main story out at you. Usually it is something aimed at getting the interest of prospective readers, so that people will buy that newspaper and not the main rival. The story is usually something amazing and unexpected, such as:

England Manager accepts England are rubbish and always have been!

Well, that may not seem so amazing to some of you, but it would certainly grab people's attention!

An advertising banner on a website is created to do almost exactly the same thing, except that instead of buying the newspaper, the user clicks on the advertising banner and is taken to the website which is being advertised. Typically, an advertising banner combines text and graphics, so the activity in this chapter will aim to achieve this. Luckily, Fireworks includes a lot of features which make the creation of an excellent advertising banner a relatively easy task.

Figure 11.1: *An advertising banner.*

What do I need to consider when I create my banner?

The skills needed for Assessment Objective 5 are almost identical to the ones you used in the last chapter to plan and create the buttons. The only difference is that, if you are targeting a **Distinction** grade, you would need to include some animation in your advertising banner.

Animation

You should know that animation means to animate or add movement. Fireworks allows you to animate objects (which have been converted to symbols) as well as text. We will look at a classic animation and then discuss other possibilities before we go on to create a practice animation.

Create a fade out animation

In this animation, one main title will fade out. We will add another title to fade in during the next section. We discussed the use of rulers and grids in Chapter 9 (Assessment Objective 3) – **Create a navigation bar or menu bar**. You might decide to use them to help you with organising the layout of your text during the next two activities.

Activity 1: Creating a fade out animation...

In this activity you will:

● learn how to make elements fade out.

(▶) Open Fireworks and create a new document 500 pixels wide and 150 pixels high.

(▶) Choose the **Text** tool. Choose **Tahoma font** and size **50**. Choose **black (#000000)** for your text colour.

(▶) Add the text **A walk in the park**. Choose the **Select** tool and drag the text so that it sits in the middle of the new Fireworks document.

(▶) Use the **Modify...Animation...Animate Selection** to bring up the animation setting interface box.

(▶) Copy the settings shown in Figure 11.2.

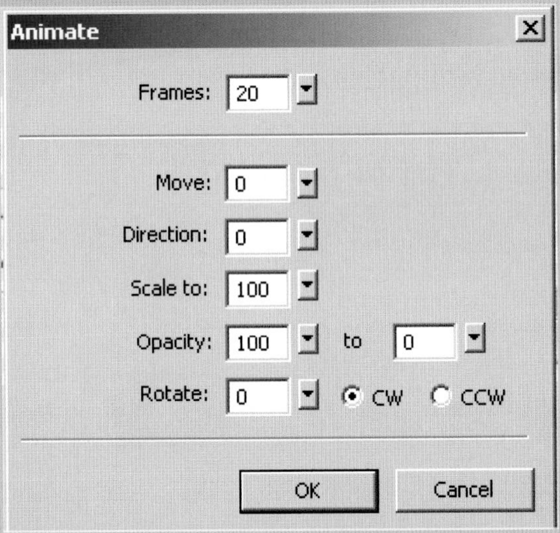

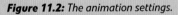

Figure 11.2: The animation settings.

(▶) Click **OK** to make your choices. A warning message will appear. Ignore this and click **OK**.

(!)TIP

By setting the Move option to 0, you have set the animation so that it is static. If, however, you wanted to make the animation physically move, you would add a figure into this option box. The animation would then move in the direction shown in the direction option box. The opacity setting controls the fade out part of the animation. By choosing 100 to 0, the graphic will fade from being fully visible, to being fully invisible over 20 Frames.

Testing the animation

Testing the animation is simply a case of hitting the play button at the bottom of the screen. Later on, we will be using the **Preview in Browser** facility.

Creating a fade in animation

We will now add another animation, so that as one piece of text disappears, another appears.

Activity 2: Creating a fade in animation...

In this activity you will:

● learn how to make elements fade in.

▶ Choose the **Text** tool. Choose **Tahoma font** and size **50**. Choose **red** for your text colour.

▶ Add the text **A way of life**. Choose the **Select** tool and drag the text so that it sits directly on top of the first piece of text.

▶ With this second piece of text selected, follow the last two steps of Activity 1 to animate this text, but this time set the **Opacity** to go from **0** to **100**.

Further animation

The animation you have just created is an excellent way of creating a **reveal**. This is basically one message coming through to replace another one. The use of different colours, as well as the animation, should attract most viewers' attention.

As well as text, you can animate objects. Try creating a simple shape with the pen tool, possibly a cross or a circle. Experiment with the settings so that the shape moves from left to right across the page and spins as it does so. Once you have done this, try fading it out.

There is one more trick you can do with an object and that is to make it spin. If you look again at **Figure 11.2,** you will see a section at the bottom which deals with **rotation**. By putting a number in the input box labelled **Rotate:**, you can set how many times your object spins during the animation. For example, if your animation lasts for 20 frames, and you set it to spin four times, it will complete a full rotation every 5 frames.

You can also set which direction the object spins. CW stands for **clockwise** (the object spins in the same direction as the second hand on a watch), whilst CCW stands for **counter clockwise** (the objects spins in the opposite direction to the second hand on a watch).

Creating the advertising banner

You will now create an advertising banner for the Les and Des website. This will combine both parts of their famous catch phrase 'A funny thing happened to me in 1973', with a graphic of both comedians shortly after their sell-out tour of piers and seaside venues in 1978. We will add the interactivity once you have created the animation.

Activity 3: Combining the graphic and animated text...

In this activity you will:

- combine text and graphics
- animate the text.

▶ Open Fireworks.

▶ Use the **File** menu to open the file **Les and Des 4.jpg**. You should have downloaded this graphic file at the beginning of this unit.

▶ Choose the **Text** tool. Choose **Tahoma font** and size **40**. Choose **black** for your text colour.

▶ Add the text **A funny thing happened to me**. Choose the **Select** tool and drag the text so that it sits directly in the middle of the graphic, but at the top. We will be animating this piece of text so that it moves down the page.

▶ Choose the text you have just added and open the animation settings interface box.

▶ Copy the settings shown in Figure 11.3.

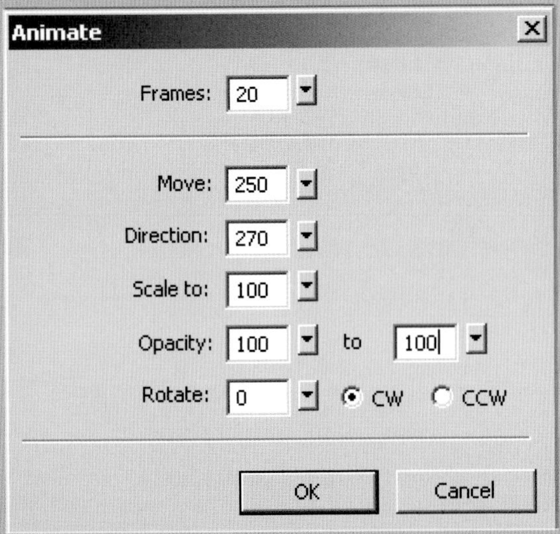

Figure 11.3: The new animation settings.

▶ Choose **Frame 16**. Do not worry about the background photograph, we will be adding that in a moment.

▶ Choose the **Text** tool. Choose **Tahoma font** and size **40**. Choose **yellow (FFFF00)** for your text colour.

▶ Add the text **in 1973**. Choose the **Select** tool and drag the text so that it sits directly in the middle of the graphic, but just below where the first piece of text will arrive at the end of the animation. We will be animating this piece of text so that it appears as the text arrives.

▶ Choose the text you have just added and open the animation settings interface box.

▶ Copy the settings shown in Figure 11.4.

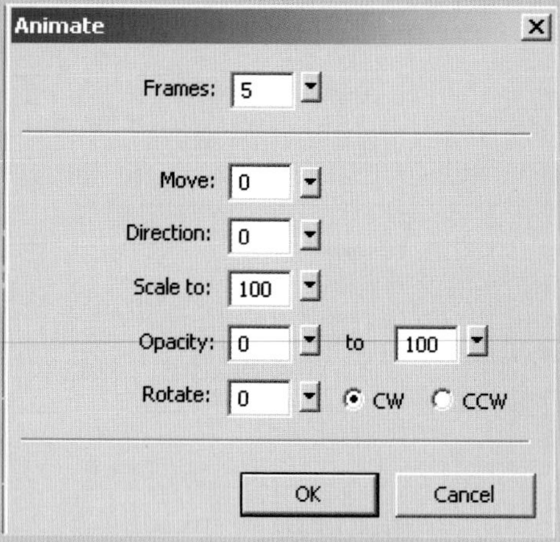

*Figure 11.4: The settings for **in 1973**.*

Finishing the job

If you now test your animation, you should see that as the first piece of text moves down the page, so the second piece appears. You might be wondering why the photograph has disappeared. If you have worked with Flash, you will not be surprised by this, as you will have realised that in order to add animation to your text, you have had to add in 19 extra frames. However, the **Les and Des 4.jpg** photograph only appears in **Frame 1**.

Activity 4: Adding the background...

In this activity you will:

* learn how to copy a background from one frame to another.

▶ Click on **Frame 1**. (If **Frame view** is not open, choose it.)

▶ Using the **Select** tool, click on the background photograph (**Les and Des 4.jpg**).

▶ Choose **Edit...Copy**.

▶ Click on **Frame 2**. Choose **Edit...Paste** to paste this photograph as the background graphic for this frame.

▶ Repeat this process for all the frames.

Saving as an animated GIF

You will need to save your file as an animated GIF. If you do not, your graphic will not be animated. It's that simple!

Activity 5: Saving as an animated GIF...

In this activity you will:

* save your file in a format for use on the Web.

▶ To save as an animated GIF, you must first **optimise** your graphic. To do so, open the **Optimise** panel. Select **Animated GIF** as the Export File Format.

Key terms

Optimising

Reducing the file size of a graphic to as small a level as possible, so that downloading speeds are improved.

Adding the interactivity

We now have to add the hyperlink. When you create your own advertising banner, you will be given a website to which to link. However, as Les Gets and Des Trunks do not really exist, we will use the address of the Heinemann website. If you would prefer, you could always use the address of a website of your choice.

Activity 6: Adding the hyperlink...

In this activity you will:

- add a hyperlink to one frame of the advertising banner
- distribute the hyperlink to all frames of the animation.

▶ With the animation you have just created open, open the **Frames and History** panel. Select any frame.

▶ Select the **Rectangle Hotspot** tool from the **Web** section of the tools panel.

▶ Create a rectangular hotspot over the whole of the graphic.

▶ Choose the **Select** tool and select the rectangular hotspot you have just created.

▶ The **Properties Inspector** will now show the properties for the hotspot. Included in these properties are the **Link** and **Alt:** for the hyperlink. Add the URL for the website to which you are linking to the **Link** field. Add suitable text to the **Alt:** field.

▶ You can preview your work by choosing **File...Preview in Browser...Preview in IEXPLORE.EXE**.

Key terms

Hotspot

A hotspot is the active (usually clickable) area of a web page or of an item of web furniture such as a banner advertisement or a navigation bar. When the mouse pointer is moved over (or clicked upon) the hotspot area, an action is performed.

Other options

Work of this quality should meet the **Distinction** criteria for Assessment Objective 5. However, you might like to go further. Other options you could explore would include animating objects as well as text, or maybe using the slicing facility to create different hotspots on the advertising banner.

CHAPTER (12)

→ *Assessment Objective 6*
Presenting Work to a Client

. . . .

Overview:

In this final chapter, we will discuss how you should present your work to a client for a specific purpose, using a suitable format for display.

How this assessment objective will be assessed...

You will be assessed on the following aspects of your website:

- the format you use to present your work
- the quality of layout and organisation of your work on the presentation
- the extent to which you use suitable file types.

Skills to use...

- You will need to present your work in a suitable format. While you could simply print your work out, this should be seen as the least impressive option.
- You will need to show that the graphics you have created have been optimised for use on the Web and have been saved in suitable formats.

How to achieve...

Pass requirements

P1 You will present work in a suitable format.

Merit requirements

M1 You will present work well in a suitable format.
M2 Your work will show the use of suitable file types.

Distinction requirements

D1 You will present work well in a suitable format.
D2 Your work will show the use of suitable file types.
D3 Graphics will be optimised for use on the Web.

Presenting your work

You should remember that if you were expecting to be paid for the work you have done, your client would be expecting to see an impressive collection of elements. If you present your work in a poor fashion, your client is less likely to be impressed, which would probably affect your chance of getting work in the future.

Unfortunately, you are probably not being paid for this work. However, this does not mean that your work does not need to be well presented. The following paragraphs give you some tips on how you might present your work.

You can choose any suitable format in which to present your work, but those listed within the specifications are:

- a web page
- a slide presentation
- printouts.

The choice of which format in which to present your work will, to some extent, depend on the skills you have for working with other software applications. However, you should consider the option to print out your completed work as the least effective and least suitable option: it does not give the user a proper flavour of the elements you have created and does not allow the user to test the elements you have created.

As the elements you have created have been specifically created for use on the World Wide Web, it would seem most appropriate that you present them as part of a web page. We will not discuss how to add these elements to web pages here, as this would require far more space than we have and is also the focus of another unit in this qualification. What we will discuss is how you can present each element to show it in the best light.

Presenting the navigation bar

The navigation bar is intended to be on each page of a website. The consistent use of a navigation bar can really create an impression of a strong house style. The best way of presenting this element would be on a number of pages in a constant position.

The choice of where on the page to place your work is, again, a matter of personal choice. However, for display purposes, placing your element at the top of the page would seem to be most appropriate.

Presenting the buttons

Buttons may be placed in any logical position on a web page. If you want to show how buttons are associated with a piece of text, then you should consider creating text on the page, so that you can show how the buttons and the text might relate. If you choose to do this, you should remember that the main focus of your work is the button and not allow the text to get in the way of showing your button to its best effect.

Presenting the advertising banner

An advertising banner is intended to draw a potential viewer into your website. Advertising banners are therefore placed on other websites and not your own. If you want to show that you have created an effective advertising banner, the best way would be to create a website to hold the navigation bar and the buttons and then link the advertising banner to this website. As you may have learnt in the unit covering the creation of websites (Unit 2), there is no need for these websites to be placed on the World Wide Web, as they may be hosted locally.

Optimising and saving work

Whichever method you choose, you must also show that you have optimised your work and saved your work using a file type suitable for use on the Web.

Optimisation is the process of making your work quick to download. In the case of animations, by far the biggest problem is the amount of frames you have to include. This is very awkward because, if you do not use enough frames, your work will not appear smooth. If you have too many, you will have a large file size and download times will be too long. As a rough guide, you should use about 10 frames for an animation.

The second issue is the choice of which file type to use. Fireworks will automatically save work in a format suitable for use on the Web. For animated elements, we have discussed saving work as **Animated GIFs** as we have worked through the tasks. If you wish to provide proof that you have saved elements in the correct format, you could either:

- provide a screenshot of the directory/folder into which you have saved your work *or*
- if you have included your work on a website, any working element must, by definition, be in a format suitable for use on the Web.

Activity 1: Creating your portfolio of web furniture...

In this activity you will:

- present your completed elements.

▶ Using the format which best suits the grade for which you are aiming, present the work you have created for Les and Des.

Index

M695